# WITHDRAWN

HOW TO ... HOW TO ... HOW TO ...

# market your
# accommodation
# business effectively

Published by VisitBritain, Thames Tower, Blacks Road, London W6 9EL
Publishing Manager: Seth Edwards
Production Manager: Celine Gale
Typesetting: Type Study, Scarborough
Printing and binding: Wace Ltd, Swindon
Cover design: Simon Russell

Front cover image courtesy of Simon Russell of Boing Graphics
Written by: Susan Briggs for VisitBritain
Additional thanks go to Pam Foden and Adrian Grinsted for taking part in
the peer group review process

ISBN – 978-0-7095-8390-5

visit **Britain**
publishing

325954

# Contents

# Introduction

The main aim of this book is to help you attract more guests to your business, whether you are running a small hotel, B&B or self-catering accommodation.

The information it contains is practical and action-oriented, so you can either use it as a reference guide or follow it step by step to develop your business.

The first two chapters explain the wider tourism environment, helping you to understand the role of the tourist boards and explaining some of the trends and changes affecting the industry.

The next chapters will help you to develop and implement a marketing action plan, and show you how to choose the most productive target markets. They guide you through the process of selecting cost-effective promotional tools, such as direct mail and PR, and then go on to consider how to create a successful website. There is also a chapter on how to reach overseas' markets.

The final chapters (Chapters 9–12) offer additional information to help you offer a high-quality product and get repeat visitors, to comply with the law and to cope with the unexpected.

# Chapter 1
# Setting the scene

This first chapter will help you to understand the tourism industry as a whole, its structure and how it works, who does what and which organisations can offer information and support. It sets the scene so you can understand the role and remit of bodies such as the tourist boards.

## The size and shape of the UK tourism industry

Tourism is a fun industry but one which can be unexpectedly complex. It is one of the largest industries in the UK, accounting for 3.5% of the UK economy and worth approximately £75 billion.

Tourism accounts for around 1.4 million jobs in the UK, which is about 5% of all people in employment. There are now more jobs in tourism than in construction or transport. A significant proportion of people working in tourism are self-employed.

There are numerous organisations that help to develop and promote tourism in Britain. These include the tourist boards as well as the travel trade.

It is important to distinguish between the three main different aspects of tourism. As the term implies, **leisure visitors** are looking for places to go in their free time and their main motivation is pleasure or a chance to be with family and friends. In this sense we are also considering people who are travelling independently rather than in an organised group. **Business** or **corporate travellers** are generally visiting other companies and frequently travel alone.

The **travel trade** are the intermediaries between you and the public. It is not easy to do, but if you can harness the power of the travel trade, you will have a ready-made sales force who can act on your behalf.

Travel agents are generally only booking agents for the tour operators whose brochures they rack. Tour operators put together packages including elements such as accommodation, sightseeing activities and transport. They may sell directly to the public or via travel agents.

Coach operators may also have their own brochures of tours or they may operate on a mainly private hire basis, simply providing a coach and driver as required by a tour operator or group travel organiser.

Incoming tour operators, handling agents and ground handlers all perform fairly similar roles, although some are more proactive than others in terms of proposing programmes to their clients instead of simply organising according to clients' requests. Their role is to take care of all the arrangements (accommodation, sightseeing, transport, guides, etc.) from the moment their overseas' clients step on to UK soil until they leave.

Group travel organisers may be working on a voluntary rather than commercial basis and organise trips on behalf of a wide range of groups and special interest clubs.

## Structure and role of the national tourist boards

This section gives an overview of the role and activities of the tourist boards and other support organisations.

The former British Tourist Authority and English Tourism Council were combined into one organisation in 2003 and renamed VisitBritain. VisitBritain now has two roles. It is responsible for promoting Britain overseas, and for promoting England to the domestic market under the Enjoy England banner. VisitBritain has a network of over 20 overseas offices and is active in more than 35 overseas' markets. It is funded by the Department for Culture, Media and Sport.

Inbound tourism makes a major contribution to the UK economy. The 30 million overseas visitors who came to the UK in 2005 spent £14.25 billion in the UK. In 2005, the UK ranked fifth in the international tourism earnings league behind the USA, Spain, France and Italy.

The size and shape of the UK tourism industry

Structure and role of the national tourist boards

The top five overseas markets for the UK in 2005 were:

| Country | Visits (000) | Country | Spend (£m) |
| --- | --- | --- | --- |
| USA | 3,438 | USA | 2,384 |
| France | 3,324 | Germany | 998 |
| Germany | 3,294 | Irish Republic | 895 |
| Irish Republic | 2,806 | France | 796 |
| Spain | 1,786 | Spain | 697 |

Inbound tourism is changing. Emerging markets such as China, Poland, Russia and South Korea are becoming more important. VisitBritain is extending its reach to maximise the potential of India, South-east Asia and Eastern Europe, the Czech Republic, Greece, Hungary, Malaysia and Thailand.

VisitBritain works in partnership with the national tourist boards in Northern Ireland, Scotland and Wales to promote an attractive image of Britain. It provides impartial tourism information and gathers essential market intelligence and insights for the UK tourism industry.

Within England, VisitBritain's key role is to encourage British residents to take additional and longer breaks in England. It does this through its Enjoy England campaigns and website **www.enjoyengland.com** and by providing central coordination for the many different organisations that promote tourism in England.

VisitBritain is not a membership organisation so you do not have to be a member to take advantage of its many tourism industry services and promotions. More information about working with VisitBritain and increasing your share of overseas' visitors is given in Chapter 8.

## New structures for regional tourist boards

There were previously nine Regional Tourist Boards (RTBs) in England but these have now been reorganised. England's nine Regional Development Agencies (RDAs) are responsible for economic development in their region and now have strategic responsibility for tourism.

The RDAs have developed new structures to manage and deliver their new tourism strategies. The approach varies from region to region.

In some areas the RTBs continue to exist as the RDA's tourism delivery partner.

In other regions the RTBs have been reconstituted as strategic bodies to oversee the work of new sub-regional organisations established by the RDAs. These are generally known as either 'Destination Management Organisations' or 'Destination Management Partnerships'.

These new-look RTBs and Destination Management Organisations receive some funding from the Department of Culture, Media and Sport, as well as membership fees from tourism companies such as accommodation providers.

If you are not already a member of your regional tourist board (or its new equivalent) you might find it useful to join. Membership benefits include promotional activities and advice. Further information about working with tourist boards is given in Chapter 7.

## Next steps – checklist

1   If you are not already a member of a regional tourist board or destination management organisation, find out how to become involved and what benefits they might offer.
2   Learn more about tourism in your area by using one of the resources listed below.

## Further information

New structures for
regional tourist boards

VisitBritain consumer website: **www.visitbritain.com**
VisitBritain corporate website:
**www.visitbritain.com/corporate**
VisitBritain industry website:
**www.visitbritain.com/ukindustry**
Enjoy England domestic consumer website:
**www.enjoyengland.com**

Next steps – checklist

VisitBritain provides a range of statistics, research,
intelligence and insights about the domestic and inbound
tourism industry at **www.visitbritain.com/research**. Other
resources include the websites **www.staruk.org.uk** and
**www.insights.org.uk**.

Further information

You can find contacts for the national and regional tourist
boards on **www.visitbritain.com/ukindustry**.

Northern Ireland Tourist Board consumer website:
**www.discovernorthernireland.com**
Northern Ireland Tourist Board tourism industry website:
**www.nitb.com**
VisitScotland consumer website: **www.visitscotland.com**
Scottish tourism industry website: **www.scotexchange.net**
Visit Wales consumer website: **www.visitwales.com**
Visit Wales industry website:
**www.industry.visitwales.co.uk**
Visit London consumer website: **www.visitlondon.com**
Visit London industry website:
**www.visitlondon.com/corporate**

UKinbound represents the interests of companies deriving a
substantial part of their income from the provision of tours
and tourism services for overseas visitors within Britain:
**www.ukinbound.org**.

## Chapter 2

# The changing face of tourism marketing

Tourism is a growth industry, so it is natural that it should be constantly changing and evolving. This section looks at some of the trends in tourism that contribute to the changing marketplace.

While some of them represent threats to current business, many can be turned to your advantage if you are able to capitalise on them. We start by looking at UK tourism now, and then consider how the market is likely to change and the trends you should know about.

### Tourism now – the current situation

The most up-to-date research data (United Kingdom Tourism Survey 2005) shows that in 2005, UK residents made over 138 million trips, amounting to around 442 million nights away from home and accounting for a spend of over £22,000 million.

Of these visits, the majority (58%) were for holiday or pleasure, with only 16% being business trips. Over 18% used their trip to combine a holiday with visiting friends and relatives. A further 26% used their trip mainly to visit friends and relatives.

The majority (65%) of UK residents make just short trips (one to three nights) within the UK. On the other hand, 35% of UK residents took a holiday of four or more nights.

Not surprisingly, the two greatest expenses incurred on holidays in the UK are accommodation and eating out. 79% of all trips are made by car. Train is the next most popular mode of transport.

The timing of trips is fairly equally distributed throughout the year, with peaks and troughs now being less marked. The third quarter (July, August and September) still accounts for the highest percentage of trips (31%), but all other quarters account for 20% to 27% of trips, with quarter one being the lowest.

Visits are spread throughout the country, although there are some predictable concentrations of visitors in traditional holiday areas.

Tourism now

– DESTINATION OF UK RESIDENTS

– BOOKING CHARACTERISTICS IN 2004

DESTINATION OF UK RESIDENTS

|  | Trips (millions) | Nights (millions) | Spend (millions) |
|---|---|---|---|
| West Midlands | 9.1 | 22.5 | 1,411 |
| East of England | 12.8 | 40.2 | 1,742 |
| East Midlands | 9.4 | 25.4 | 1,216 |
| London | 10.7 | 24.2 | 1,968 |
| North West | 15.3 | 44.1 | 2,551 |
| North Wales | 3.6 | 13.6 | 589 |
| North East | 4.6 | 13.5 | 822 |
| South East | 18.2 | 51.6 | 2,483 |
| South West | 21.3 | 83.6 | 3,609 |
| Yorkshire | 11.9 | 35.2 | 1,694 |
| Total England | 113.3 | 340.3 | 17,496 |

(*Source*: United Kingdom Tourism Survey 2005)

It is interesting to consider the ways in which bookings were made, particularly in view of the very high number of survey respondents who said they did not make a booking. The booking statistics overleaf demonstrate booking habits in the previous year (2004).

BOOKING CHARACTERISTICS IN 2004

|  | UK residents (millions) |
| --- | --- |
| Firm booking via the internet | 13.0 |
| Firm booking made in person | 6.0 |
| Firm booking via the telephone | 31.5 |
| Firm booking via E-mail | 2.3 |
| Firm booking via post | 1.5 |
| Firm booking made in another way | 0.7 |
| No booking | 70.7 |
| Don't know | 0.6 |
| All trips | 126.6 |

(*Source*: United Kingdom Tourism Survey 2004)

## What does this mean for you?

You are most likely to attract guests who want to stay with you as part of their holiday or short break, but a proportion may be willing to use your accommodation in order to visit their friends and relatives. Depending on the area in which you operate, it might be worth investing in local marketing as well as advertising further afield.

There is little point in expecting visitors to stay with you for a full week or more. Most domestic visitors prefer short breaks, although you might be able to persuade them to stay one more night.

Domestic visitors spend a significant amount on eating out. Perhaps you can convince them to eat in your restaurant if you have one. Guests will appreciate accurate and appropriate information about local restaurants and pubs that serve food. Offering strong local knowledge is one way of encouraging guests to return.

It will be interesting to look at the next phase of research relating to booking methods, at a time when we would expect the number of internet bookings to increase. Considering how new this method is, it is surprising how well established it already is. Having a good and easy-to-use website is imperative.

## Tourism market trends – how the market is changing

### CHANGES IN AVAILABLE LEISURE TIME

Over the past 50 years or so the tourism industry has developed rapidly. Incomes have risen, travel has become cheaper and most people have benefited from longer holiday entitlements and shorter working weeks.

Conversely, many full-time professionals are now working longer than ever before. Work pressure and job insecurity make people less likely to take long holidays, but more likely to take a series of short breaks so they are away from work for shorter periods of time. Such people are likely to be *cash rich,* but *time poor.* They may actually pay more for a shorter break.

People with limited time want to ensure they get *value for time* as well as value for money, often being willing to pay more to guarantee a better experience. This is why offering a high-quality product is essential.

### DEMOGRAPHIC CHANGES

People who have already retired are likely to live longer and have a higher disposable income than their counterparts several years ago. Governments are, however, now recommending *raising* retirement ages in the future in order to counteract the effects of an ageing population. Over the next 10 years there will be a large increase in the number of people in Britain aged 65 or over. By the year 2015 they will outnumber the under 16s for the first time.

This is good news for tourism. The older population is likely to be more active, in better health and have a higher disposable income than previous generations. They want to travel and enjoy their leisure time. They will have higher-quality expectations.

Tourism now
- DESTINATION OF UK RESIDENTS
- BOOKING CHARACTERISTICS IN 2004

What does this mean for you?

Tourism market trends
- CHANGES IN AVAILABLE LEISURE TIME
- DEMOGRAPHIC CHANGES
- LIFESTYLE CHANGES
- THE CHALLENGE OF SUSTAINABLE TOURISM
- CHANGES IN THE WAY WE BOOK OUR HOLIDAYS
- NEW OVERSEAS' MARKETS
- GROWTH IN ADDITIONAL HOLIDAYS AND SHORT BREAKS
- MORE DISCERNING CONSUMERS

### LIFESTYLE CHANGES

There is an increased trend towards holidays and short breaks that lead to some form of self-development or improvement. The Germans previously led the way in this market, with a marked turn away from purely sun–sea–sand holidays towards study tours during which they have an opportunity to learn something about the destination and culture. This does not mean that they have abandoned sun destinations, but that they also look for a more in-depth experience of the host country. This move is now being followed by other nationalities.

Short breaks are being used as a chance to learn new skills or sample new activities. These could be adrenalin sports, gentler hobbies such as painting, or simple retreats.

This development will lead to increased segmentation of holiday motivations and different types of holiday. For example, we can already identify packages which focus on sports tourism, health spas and relaxation, food and drink, heritage and films. Some accommodation providers have yet to capitalise on this trend in order to extend their season and reduce troughs in occupancy levels.

### THE CHALLENGE OF SUSTAINABLE TOURISM

There is a growing awareness of the impact of visitors on host destinations. Sustainable tourism is becoming more important. Visitors recognise that tourism can have negative as well as positive effects and are becoming more interested in ensuring that their visit does not degrade the resources of the area which they are visiting.

Considering the need for sustainability and developing good green tourism practices can be good for the environment *and* your business.

### CHANGES IN THE WAY WE BOOK OUR HOLIDAYS

One of the most dramatic changes in tourism has been the increase in independent holidays. Fewer people now book through traditional high street travel agents.

The internet is becoming increasingly important and is responsible for two additional trends. There is a greater desire for instant gratification in that we now expect to receive information and responses almost immediately. Accommodation providers who cannot offer online booking may be passed over in preference for another who can immediately confirm a booking.

There is also increasing use of internet comparison and review sites. Visitors no longer rely on a sole source of information. Before making their accommodation booking, they may use a variety of other sites including official tourist board sites and review sites such as **www.tripadvisor.com**. As time is so precious, visitors want to be certain that the place they have chosen is really suitable.

### NEW OVERSEAS' MARKETS

Changing political and economic situations mean that you now need to be aware of new emerging markets, such as Russia, China and India.

Low-cost airlines, such as Ryanair and easyJet, are making it easier for visitors from a wider range of overseas' markets to come to Britain. At the same time there is added competition from new destinations for the UK's tourism product. Travellers are fickle and always looking for the next fashionable destination.

### GROWTH IN ADDITIONAL HOLIDAYS AND SHORT BREAKS

Although holiday-taking by the British has increased over the past two decades, there has been a marked change in our choice of destination. The norm was to take a week or two-week long holiday at a seaside destination in Britain.

There have been changes in terms of holiday length, particularly with the growth of short breaks, but also in terms of where we take these holidays. Short holidays and short breaks (i.e. up to four days) in Britain have grown, whereas the growth in long holidays has all been channelled into holidays abroad.

There has been growth in *additional* holiday-taking. This means that increased numbers take a long holiday abroad and then at least one short break in the UK. Compared to holidays as a whole, these additional holidays tend to be less

Tourism market trends
- CHANGES IN AVAILABLE LEISURE TIME
- DEMOGRAPHIC CHANGES
- LIFESTYLE CHANGES
- THE CHALLENGE OF SUSTAINABLE TOURISM
- CHANGES IN THE WAY WE BOOK OUR HOLIDAYS
- NEW OVERSEAS' MARKETS
- GROWTH IN ADDITIONAL HOLIDAYS AND SHORT BREAKS
- MORE DISCERNING CONSUMERS

seasonal, less likely to be spent at the seaside, more likely to be activity-based, and make more use of serviced accommodation.

### MORE DISCERNING CONSUMERS

The increased choice of destinations and types of accommodation means that consumers are becoming more discerning. They are demanding better quality. The days of bad tempered landladies shooing guests out of their guesthouse for the day are thankfully long gone.

VisitBritain and other organisations such as the Automobile Association have been working to remove some of the confusion about accommodation-grading systems in order to make them easier to understand. Greater publicity for the new harmonised schemes will raise public awareness and demand for quality-assessed accommodation. Accommodation which is not inspected and assessed is less likely to be featured in tourist board promotional activities.

## Challenges for the future

It will become increasingly important to be aware of and cater for cultural differences. We will not be able to develop new international markets without fully understanding their needs.

Consumers will continue to be faced with a bewildering array of choices and destinations. Grabbing and keeping their attention will only get more difficult.

As stress grows, visitors are likely to seek out less frenetic and more escapist destinations. They will be willing to travel to find exactly the right quality and experience.

There will be increased competition from newer destinations that are eager to please, offering high-quality products for much cheaper prices than in Britain. We will need to convince and explain to visitors that what we offer is truly unique and only to be found in Britain.

## Next steps – checklist

1 Think how you can differentiate your product and take advantage of the trend towards self-development by suggesting activities that guests could do during a short break. You could simply provide a list of suitable activities or extensive information within your website, or you might like to combine efforts with a local activity centre or artist and undertake some joint marketing.

2 Many guests look for inspirational suggestions. How can you provide new ideas for holidays and short breaks? Can you take advantage of specific markets and interests?

3 As you will see in the next chapter, all accommodation providers need to find something which sets them apart from others and makes them more distinctive. You could consider ways to make your accommodation 'greener' and more environmentally friendly in order to cater for the increasing number of guests who are more environmentally aware.

4 It is essential that you have a high-quality and persuasive website. If you do not already offer it, online booking could make all the difference to your business. Consider how VisitBritain's EnglandNet project could help you – see Chapter 6, about web marketing.

5 Try to encourage guests to leave positive comments on some of the review sites and make sure you increase visitors to your website by optimising your website for the various search engines.

6 Be aware of any changes taking place in your area, such as increased numbers of visitors from particular overseas' markets. Your regional tourist board should be able to provide information about trends and developments in your area.

7 If there is an airport near you used by any of the low-cost airlines, find out which routes they serve and investigate if it is worth promoting to those markets.

8 Take a fresh look at your accommodation. Are there any aspects that you could upgrade or improve in order to provide a better service for more discerning customers?

Tourism market trends

– CHANGES IN AVAILABLE LEISURE TIME
– DEMOGRAPHIC CHANGES
– LIFESTYLE CHANGES
– THE CHALLENGE OF SUSTAINABLE TOURISM
– CHANGES IN THE WAY WE BOOK OUR HOLIDAYS
– NEW OVERSEAS' MARKETS
– GROWTH IN ADDITIONAL HOLIDAYS AND SHORT BREAKS
– MORE DISCERNING CONSUMERS

Challenges for the future

Next steps – checklist

Further information

If your accommodation is not already quality inspected, you are strongly advised to consider participating in the new schemes. More details are given in Chapter 9.

## Further information

The VisitBritain industry website has details of current research, statistics and trends: **www.visitbritain.com/ukindustry**. You can also find more information on **www.staruk.org.uk**.

Keep up to date with the latest trends and business ideas by subscribing to free newsletters on sites such as **www.springwise.com** and **www.trendwatching.com**.

'Green tourism' is a term used to describe best environmental practice within the tourism sector. The Green Tourism Business Scheme asks businesses to agree to a code of conduct, and through independent assessment of their activities, members make a commitment towards reducing the impact of their business on the environment. For more details see **www.green-business.co.uk**.

The Green Audit Guide is designed to be used by all types of tourism businesses. It contains practical ideas to help benefit from the attraction of the countryside at the same time as contributing to the local community and economy and protecting the environment. A free copy can be downloaded from **www.greenauditkit.org**.

# Chapter 3
# Plan now: save money later

This chapter considers how to plan your marketing and develop a marketing action plan. Some accommodation providers prefer to just 'get on with it' without sitting down and writing a plan first of all, but this can mean wasting money. Even if you only spend a couple of hours planning your marketing in advance, you will make it more effective, better coordinated and less costly.

The chapter starts with an introduction to the essentials of marketing. It will help you to assess your strengths and weaknesses, and most importantly, suggest ways to improve on them. It will help you to develop a Unique Selling Point (USP) and work out how you can compete in today's marketplace.

## What is marketing?

Most marketing is common sense. All you have to do to make money is sell the right product at the right price to the right people in the right way. Of course, getting this combination right is not always easy. Probably the two most important aspects of marketing are targeting and making the best use of appropriate promotional tools. Spending just a short time thinking about what you are selling will help you to get this right.

For many years, we have talked about marketing as being about the four 'Ps':

**Product:** what you are selling, including ways in which your product or service is better than competitors';

**Price:** what you charge for your service, varying according to demand and other factors;

**Place:** this does not mean where you are, but the marketplace or the way your guests make a booking or find out about you;

**Promotion:** how you sell your product, including the messages and tools you will use to promote your product, such as brochures, letters and advertisements. This is usually the most interesting and practical aspect of marketing!

Most people would add a fifth 'P': **people**. Your staff and the way you interact with guests is an essential addition and could make as much difference to the way your accommodation is perceived as the price or your promotional activities.

## Why bother to plan?

Marketing is essentially a *process*, rather than a series of scattered and isolated activities. Planning focuses your attention and gives you the opportunity to set targets. It means you will be able to develop better methods of evaluating results so you do not spend money unnecessarily. Scheduling and coordinating all marketing activities will make them more effective and save you money. For example, if you are placing any advertising, it makes sense to increase your PR activities at the same time in order to maximise that investment.

Once you have developed your marketing action plan, you may need to undertake a little internal organisation to get staff to help you, or at least to communicate to other staff what you plan to do so that you are all 'pulling in the same direction'.

## WHAT SHOULD A MARKETING PLAN INCLUDE?
Marketing plans should ideally include the following key components:

What is marketing?

Why bother to plan?

– WHAT SHOULD A
   MARKETING PLAN
   INCLUDE?

*Current situation*
This should include a brief review of the 'product' or service you offer, analysis of your target markets and any important trends.

*Marketing objectives*
This will involve setting some basic targets and defining what you want to achieve. You will also need to decide how you are going to monitor your performance.

*SWOT analysis*
You will need to consider the factors that are likely to make you succeed or fail, looking both inside and outside your company. SWOT stands for **Strengths**, **Weaknesses**, **Opportunities** and **Threats**.

*Competitor analysis*
You will need to decide who your competitors are, what they are doing and how you can compete with them.

*Unique Selling Point*
This is the one aspect of your accommodation or service that differentiates you from your competitors.

*Market research*
How much do you really know about your existing and potential guests? Before you can move forward you will need to establish basic information about them.

*Target markets*
It is much more cost-effective to target just a few strong markets than to adopt a 'something for everyone' approach, so you will need to choose which markets are most worthwhile and important to you.

*Promotional tools*
You will need to develop a sort of shopping list of the promotional tools you will use and what budget you will devote to them. Promotional tools could include advertising, PR, personal selling, website, etc.

There is a marketing action plan checklist at the end of this chapter so you can make sure you have covered each of these areas in your marketing plan before looking in more detail at promotional activities.

You will probably find that as you develop each element of the marketing plan, you might need to go back and change some other sections. This is quite normal, and is actually the sign of a good marketing plan, which should be adapted as situations change and constantly re-evaluated.

## Current situation

This does not need to be a long section, but it should give an overview of three main areas:

1  The 'product' you are trying to sell.
2  Current markets.
3  Trends that might affect your business.

### 1 YOUR 'PRODUCT'

Asking 'What am I really selling?' may seem like a strange question, but is actually a very good starting point. You need to know what makes you different from every other hotel in your area. A useful exercise is to consider the features, advantages and benefits of what you offer.

The **features** are physical characteristics. The **advantages** are offered by or included in the features and the **benefits** are what can be gained from those advantages. Many accommodation providers list their features, but guests buy *benefits*, not features.

Let us use the example of a small hotel. When asked what sort of hotel they have, most hoteliers will respond by listing their features. They might say that they have 20 bedrooms. Some might go on to explain the advantages of those features, such as the en-suite facilities and quiet location. The hoteliers who really attract guests are those who make the benefits more explicit. These might include 'rest, relaxation and privacy'.

Consider which hotel you would prefer to stay in. Would you book the one whose brochure says, 'We have 20 bedrooms with en-suite bathrooms, in a good location' or one which says, 'You will feel relaxed and refreshed, enjoying the fresh air and tranquillity at Hotel Bliss'? Most people are more interested in what the facilities will actually mean to them.

The key to success is selling **experiences** and **benefits** rather than features.

Remember that even a simple overnight stay in a Bed and Breakfast is an experience. A good one-night stay in a B&B is made up of several components: good and easy-to-find location, a warm welcome, comfort and style of the bedroom and bathroom, and quality of the breakfast. The way that breakfast is served and any interaction with the staff is part of the 'experience'.

Why bother to plan?

– WHAT SHOULD A MARKETING PLAN INCLUDE?

Current situation

– 1 YOUR 'PRODUCT'
– 2 YOUR CURRENT MARKETS
– 3 TRENDS THAT MIGHT AFFECT YOUR BUSINESS

---

### What are you selling?

Take a moment to think about what you offer. This will vary, depending on whether your hotel caters for business or leisure travellers.

Do you offer a chance to relax? Or guaranteed efficiency? Can you promise a comfortable bed or quiet rooms? Do you have some of the friendliest staff in the area? Perhaps you have the smartest hotel or the cosiest B&B? What are the benefits to your guests? Why should they stay with you?

Jot down some of the benefits of staying in your accommodation.

---

### 2 YOUR CURRENT MARKETS

You should already have a reasonable idea of who books your accommodation. It is often easier to attract more of the same type of people than to tackle completely new markets. This is because you know they already enjoy what you have to offer and you presumably understand their needs.

You need to find out where guests come from and how they travel. Knowing about their average age, income group, lifestyle and interests will all help you to decide where to advertise. If you find it difficult to answer these questions, you should make a note to conduct some customer research as soon as possible. You can do this informally by simply speaking to your guests. There is more information about choosing target markets in Chapter 4.

---

### Decide who your customers are

Ask yourself the following questions:

- Where do your guests come from? How far do they travel to stay with you?
- Are they all of a similar age or stage in their lives or very different; for example, couples with young families or middle-aged business people? Perhaps you have different types of guests on different days of the week?
- What sort of parties do they travel in: are they in couples, families, small groups of friends or colleagues, tour groups, etc.?
- How would you describe their income group and lifestyle? Describing an average day in someone's life is often a good way of finding out what 'makes them tick' and what benefits you can offer them. For example, a stressed mum with young children would love to relax, whereas a busy business traveller wants efficient and quick service.
- How do they generally hear about you and make their bookings? Who or what influences their decisions?

Try to write down the answers to these questions now. If you find this difficult to do you might need to invest in some market research.

---

## 3 TRENDS THAT MIGHT AFFECT YOUR BUSINESS

As Chapter 2 showed, this is a changing marketplace. Are there any particular trends that will affect you? Are there any changes in your local area? Make it your business to keep up to date with what is happening where you are, as well as in the wider world.

Current situation

– 1 YOUR 'PRODUCT'

– 2 YOUR CURRENT
   MARKETS

– 3 TRENDS THAT
   MIGHT AFFECT YOUR
   BUSINESS

---

### Decide which trends might affect you

You need to keep abreast of trends and likely changes all the time, whether through the media or through customer feedback.

Take a moment now to jot down any trends you have noticed recently.

What action could you take to make sure you either benefit from these trends or to mitigate any negative effects?

---

## Marketing objectives

Marketing objectives

It will be hard to assess the effectiveness of your marketing activities and measure your performance unless you set some objectives in the form of tangible targets. You will also need to set a clear timetable for your activities.

Most accommodation providers prefer to set sales or profit-oriented targets. For example, you might like to achieve a 10% increase on sales over the next 12 months, or gain a 20% increase on current occupancy levels by focusing on sales during the traditionally 'difficult' months of January and February.

Whatever objectives you choose, you will need to ensure they are measurable, include a time period, are realistic and in line with general market trends and demands. Try to make them as specific as possible, as they are easier to measure and you will find them more motivating.

There are several ways of evaluating your marketing efforts in addition to considering actual performance against the objectives set. You might also choose to measure bookings or requests for information and conversion rates weekly, monthly or quarterly, and look at periods of major marketing activity to see if they had the desired effect.

---

**Setting your objectives and deciding what you want to achieve**

What will your objectives be? When will you review your performance?

Write down what your objectives will be and when you will renew how successful you have been. Put this date in your diary now!

---

## SWOT analysis

A SWOT analysis looks at the **Strengths**, **Weaknesses**, **Opportunities** and **Threats** facing your company or product.

Many organisations use a SWOT analysis as the first step in developing their marketing plan, perhaps because it is a relatively easy process, so a good place to start. It is a useful audit and helps to focus the mind, but is only effective if followed up by consideration of the points it raises and by actual plans on how to use the findings.

The strengths and weaknesses relate to internal factors, some of which can be influenced or changed. The opportunities and threats are external factors, which often cannot be changed.

Once you have conducted a SWOT analysis you will be able to consider how you can make the most of the strengths and opportunities you have identified, and what you can do to minimise the weaknesses and threats. These findings should be integrated into the marketing plan.

Here are some of the aspects you should be looking at. Do not just restrict yourself to looking at these points. Using a team approach and 'brain-storming' together is a useful way of conducting a SWOT analysis; write everything down and think about it later. You may find that some things which you consider strengths could also be seen as weaknesses.

Marketing objectives

SWOT analysis

– ACTION POINTS FOR
  SWOT ANALYSIS

## Strengths

**Your location:** is it easily accessible, convenient, obvious and simple to find?

**Staff:** are they professional and friendly? Do they have some special skills such as languages that make you superior to your competitors?

**Service:** do you offer a good level of service or comfort, or perhaps an unusually broad range of services?

**Marketing:** do you have a high profile, strong established market or use innovative marketing methods?

## Weaknesses

**Your location:** perhaps it is the reverse of the above?

**Reputation and image:** could it be better?

**Staff:** do they need more training or perhaps you have staff shortages?

**Services:** could they be more efficient or better in some way?

**Internal problems:** these could include bad organisation, or reactive instead of proactive management.

## Opportunities

**Trends or fashions:** consider, for example, the increased interest in certain activities, such as golf or walking.

**Changes in population:** can you take advantage of the fact that more senior citizens are living longer, with a greater disposable income?

continued

**Developments:** are you making the best of technological changes, like the expansion of the internet?

**Promotional opportunities:** look for campaigns in which you could participate, such as those offered by VisitBritain, targeting a particular market.

Threats

**Competition:** what are your competitors up to? Perhaps there are some new developments which might affect your business?

**Economic effects:** consider whether there is a recession, high inflation or unemployment, for example.

**Developments:** changes may be negative as well as positive, such as the threat of terrorist attacks.

For each of the strengths, weaknesses, opportunities and threats you list, you need to consider what actions you might take to help maximise the strengths and opportunities, and minimise the weaknesses and threats.

### MAKING SURE YOU INCLUDE ACTION POINTS FOR YOUR SWOT ANALYSIS

It is important to include action points in your SWOT analysis. For example, you might say that your quiet location is a strength. An action point for this would be to make sure that every piece of promotional information, from your brochure to your website, stresses the benefits of that quiet location.

You might say that actually finding your accommodation is a weakness and can be a bit of a challenge. An action point from that would be to ensure that all guests are sent out good clear directions, that you improve the maps on your website and in your brochure, and you look at how to make the signage to your property clearer and easier to follow.

> ## Seeing the bigger picture with a SWOT analysis
>
> Spend an hour or so with some colleagues conducting a quick SWOT analysis using the questions on page 23.
>
> Once you have answered all the questions, go through them again and consider what you will do next. How will you maximise the strengths and opportunities? How will you maximise the weaknesses and threats?

SWOT analysis

– ACTION POINTS FOR SWOT ANALYSIS

## Competitor analysis

Competitor analysis

You will probably already have some awareness of your local competitors. It is worth taking an extra look around your area and on the internet to double-check who your competitors might be. You can save time and money by keeping a keen eye on their activities, and learning by their successes and failures.

Make a telephone enquiry and/or E-mail enquiry to some of your competitors to find out how they respond, have a look at their promotional materials and learn more about their services. If you think they might recognise your name or voice, you might want to ask a friend to help.

If some of your competitors offer cheaper rates than you, do not automatically be tempted to lower yours. You do not have to be the cheapest to compete more effectively. Some people are put off by prices which appear too cheap: value for money is more attractive.

Remember that not all your competitors will be in the immediate locality. Some of them will be in other areas, but can be considered competitors because they target a similar market or offer similar facilities.

It helps if you make a conscious effort to carry out a fairly formal analysis every few months, jotting down your findings so you can decide how you will use the information.

## What are your competitors up to and how can you beat them?

Here is a list of questions to help assess your competitors:

**First impressions:** how do they answer the telephone? Quickly and politely or as if it is too much effort? What does their signage and entrance look like – how do you think their customers perceive them?

**Pricing:** do they offer value for money? How do they present their prices?

**Promotional material:** if you asked for some information to be sent to you, how long did it take? Is the information complete? Could you learn from the format or design?

**Who are their customers?** If it's possible to actually see their customers, you can learn a lot about them by assessing their age groups, people they are travelling with (for example, do you see a lot of family groups or single people?), cars, clothes, etc. Is this exactly the same market as yours or a different one? If it is the same one, you can compete by learning more about your customers and what they want, and ensuring your promotional activities convey this message. If your competitors attract a different market, should you target it too? How are your markets different?

**Their marketing activities:** few of us would recognise the difference between standard grocery products bought at two different supermarkets. It is the image and marketing of the supermarkets that makes the difference. In the same way you may find that competing hotels are similar to you but promote their accommodation very differently.

When you have done all this you should be able to draw up a list of your closest competitors, looking at their prices, the way they welcome guests, facilities and promotional activities.

Analyse each of these aspects and decide where you lag behind or are stronger. What are you going to do about it?

# Unique Selling Point

If someone asks you what makes your accommodation special, what do you say? Can you immediately respond with a compelling reason to stay with you instead of your competitors? A Unique Selling Point (USP) is something that makes you stand out from your competitors: something that makes you better or different from them. There are basically three ways of competing which are described below.

### COMPETING ON PRICE

Some companies focus heavily on controlling their costs, which allows them to keep prices down and compete on price. Probably the best known examples of this are the low-cost airlines who offer a good but 'no frills' service. This is not the same as simply offering a cheap product which might be of much lower quality. 'Cheap' and 'value for money' are not the same.

For some accommodation providers, competing on price is a sound strategy, providing they can still be profitable. You should also be aware that competitors could always choose to undercut your prices and then you would be left without a strong USP.

If you do compete on price, at some point customers will either begin to suspect you offer an inferior service or ask for further discounts. During a recession or downturn many hotels will offer special discounts, but then there is always the danger that guests will cease to value the product at its *real* price.

Some companies choose to compete on price without being the cheapest. By developing a reputation for excellence, it is sometimes possible to demand higher prices. Remember the Stella Artois 'reassuringly expensive' advertisements?

### DIFFERENTIATED APPROACH

A differentiated approach relies on having a 'unique' (in the original rather than promotional sense of the word) product or offering a truly superior service.

Competitor analysis

Unique Selling Point
- COMPETING ON PRICE
- DIFFERENTIATED APPROACH
- FOCUSED OR NICHE APPROACH

In the tourism industry, *reputation* goes a long way towards this. Perhaps more than any other industry, tourism is not one which just relies on individual components. Most tourism products are made up of several inter-related ingredients, which together deliver a total **experience**.

A guesthouse may have the same number of bedrooms and basic services as its neighbour, but is somehow made different by less tangible elements: the view from bedroom windows, a pleasant garden, cosy lounge or warm welcome from the owners.

In this sense a differentiated approach is made possible. The basic elements of a tourism product or service may appear very similar, but they can be brought together in different ways to develop an experience which is vastly different from competitors'. This could mean a quicker service, one which is easier to book, an all-inclusive price or a warmer welcome.

The differentiated approach relies on excellent customer service and creative marketing to stay ahead of competitors. The most important factor is identifying key strengths and highlighting them.

### FOCUSED OR NICHE APPROACH

A focused approach means concentrating on particular *markets* or *niches*, understanding their needs completely and developing products and promotions that are completely appropriate for those markets. This approach requires an excellent knowledge of the chosen markets. It is equally important to anticipate changes in the marketplace as well as demands for new products and services.

A focused approach is often used by smaller companies without massive resources but with an excellent understanding of their target markets. Instead of using an 'all things to all people' or 'something for everyone' approach, they can operate within niche markets that are too small to attract the 'big boys'.

Smaller companies can develop closer and more direct relationships with their clients, so a focused approach is particularly suitable. Concentrating on a limited number of markets is also more cost-effective. A good example of this is a well-known country house hotel in the West Country. It is close to several other country house hotels but manages to have a higher profile because it has a very specific main market, catering for affluent couples with their children and offering appropriate services.

Unique Selling Point

– COMPETING ON PRICE

– DIFFERENTIATED
  APPROACH

FOCUSED OR NICHE
APPROACH

---

### Finding what makes you better than your competitors

You need to decide what your Unique Selling Point is. Answering some of these questions should help you to define it.

- What makes your product/service better or different?
- What are the benefits of it to your guests?
- How are you offering exactly what your guests need?
- Why should anyone book your accommodation rather than your competitors'?
- Are you going to compete on price, by being better/different, or by focusing on niche markets?

---

## Market research

Market research

Knowledge is power. Marketing is about understanding the needs of your target markets. Research can help you to do this, whether you conduct it formally or informally.

There are basically two different types of research: **quantitative** and **qualitative**.

Quantitative surveys seek specific answers which are often presented in statistical form, such as '25% of visitors to London said they would return'. Quantitative surveys generate statistical information, answering questions such as 'who?, 'where?' and 'when?' This kind of research is particularly useful for monitoring changes and development. For example, a hotel that wishes to carry out 'Welcome Host' training might decide to conduct a guest survey before and after the training session to try to gauge its effect.

### Case study – Loch View Hotel

*Developing a profitable business through niche marketing*

Loch View Hotel in Scotland is a three-star hotel with a wide range of leisure facilities, perched on the edge of one of the Scottish Lochs. It is open for only part of the year, from Easter to the end of October, so needs to maximise occupancy levels within a relatively short season. Occupancy is around 85% during the peak English school holiday months of July and August, with much lower occupancy outside these times.

The hotel is profitable but there is increased competition from other hotels in the area, including some of the newer budget-style operations. Loch View Hotel has a full range of leisure services to appeal to adults, and an equally good selection of activities and services for children. In addition to providing baby-listening services in each room, children's activity packs and a children's storytelling session in the evening (so that parents can enjoy a later dinner alone), it offers freshly cooked organic children's meals, prams for hire, nappies, and so on.

Marketing activities tended to be quite sporadic, relying on when the owners had time to undertake promotional activities, often induced by panic at times of low occupancy. As competition increased from other family-oriented destinations, such as Euro Disney and Center Parcs, they realised that they needed to take advice and develop a more systematic approach to marketing.

Loch View already benefited from an excellent reputation and word-of-mouth recommendations from previous guests. A SWOT analysis showed that the hotel already had a strong USP, which was not being fully promoted. The owners of Loch View already offered many added-value services, such as free

continued

emergency supplies of nappies, sauna, gym and leisure facilities, games, and so on, but were not promoting them in their own right, seeing such facilities as simply 'part of the service'. This meant that potential guests were not necessarily aware of these services, and made unfavourable comparisons on paper between Loch View and other cheaper accommodation because they did not see what was included.

The owners also realised that they already had an important niche market – professional people, often late parents, who wanted a holiday that both they and their children enjoyed. Many hotels that offer special meals for children rely on standard menus such as chicken nuggets and chips, and beefburgers and chips. Loch View Hotel offers imaginative, well-presented and healthy meals which many parents would rather feed to their children.

They also do not 'penalise' parents by lowering the standard of adult meals. Within the restaurant, there are separate areas for adults dining alone and those with young children. Services such as the storytelling hour also make it easier for parents to enjoy some time alone.

The leisure facilities for adults were not fully promoted. The owners of Loch View realised that they could offer other added-value services such as massages to make parents feel pampered, and which would also appeal to adults without children.

Informal research among existing guests showed that the trigger for many family stays at the hotel was 'pester power' – children who saw some of the information in the brochure or who remembered an earlier visit. There also seemed to be the opportunity to encourage existing guests to return for a short break at non-peak periods.

continued

A secondary market was seen to be short breaks for adults without children, who were looking for an activity holiday or simply a chance to relax and use the leisure facilities. However, some of the latter wanted to be certain that the hotel could cater for them and was not solely child-oriented, even though they did not necessarily mind that there would be children in the hotel.

As a result of this research and clearer focus the owners of Loch View Hotel took three important steps:

- They developed a range of short breaks. Some of these were children-oriented and focused on current crazes and children's interests, such as treasure hunts looking for miniature versions of popular TV characters. A children's club was initiated with special benefits for repeat guests. Other short breaks targeted adults, with ideas for pampering and special interest weekends. Similar ideas were used to build midweek business by targeting active retired 'empty nesters' who are free to travel at any time and who may react to triggers such as special interest breaks.
- When it was time to reprint the brochure, a supplement was developed which was aimed purely at children, using some of the pictures drawn by guests, and focusing on the wide range of children's facilities. This meant that while the main brochure mentioned the children's facilities, it was also possible to mail just the main brochure to adults without children to stress the range of adult leisure facilities.
- They developed a programme of PR activities to raise the profile of the hotel, often using some of the short breaks as the hook or story for the press so that they could target special interest publications.

continued

With the help of a PR agency, Loch View Hotel was also able to generate publicity with other angles such as:

- light-hearted 'fillers', such as surveys about what parents say they most need on holiday with their children, statistics about the numbers of stories told over the season during the storytelling hour and the favourites, most popular children's dishes, etc.;
- launch of each new short break or special interest programme;
- launch of the new children's brochure, with a photo-call including some of the children who had contributed artwork;
- innovations such as asking children rather than adults to complete guest satisfaction questionnaires.

Using this approach enabled the Loch View Hotel to target special interest publications and to promote holidays separately to parents and non-parents. However, they also had to be careful to ensure that they were able to balance the needs of parents and non-parents. For example, they did not offer 'perfect peace' at times when it was likely that the hotel would be full of children!

Thanks to a more sustained and structured approach to marketing, the Loch View Hotel has been successful in promoting itself to a wide range of special interest publications which have frequently used the angles listed above. Other promotional activities have included using vouchers to stimulate word-of-mouth recommendations and to encourage guests to return during off-peak periods. Direct mail has been particularly effective, especially with the introduction of the separate children's brochure.

*The location and name of this hotel has been changed to preserve commercial confidentiality.*

Qualitative research seeks to find out people's personal reactions and feelings about products or experiences. It is particularly useful when developing marketing campaigns and for motivational research, asking why or how customers made the decision to purchase (or not purchase) certain products.

Research does not necessarily involve interviewing people face to face or **primary** research. If you need general information about one of your markets, you can probably use **desk** or **secondary** research. This uses existing reports and published sources. You can, for example, find descriptions of key overseas' markets within the Marketing Intelligence section of VisitBritain's industry website.

You might decide to develop your own in-house questionnaire or survey. You can increase response rates and the accuracy of the feedback by following a few simple rules. Don't make questions too difficult or complex, or include two questions in one. Avoid loading them so it is difficult to respond honestly. Read your questions carefully to make sure they are not ambiguous. As you draft the questionnaire, think about how you will use it. You can avoid it becoming too long by thinking in advance what you will do with each of the responses.

Beware of making the questionnaire too long and making it into a memory test – ask only about recent decisions and experiences. You should also remember to explain the purpose of the questionnaire at the beginning and thank the respondent at the end.

Closed questions that require only a yes/no response are quickest to answer and evaluate but do not give very detailed information. Open questions such as 'who?' or 'why?' elicit more descriptive and useful statements, but there may be a lower response rate.

You will probably get a high response rate if you include multiple-choice questions because they are relatively quick and easy to complete.

Before you print hundreds of copies, test your
questionnaire on friends and colleagues to see how easy it is
to answer, and check that the responses will not be 'skewed'
by the way you have set the questions. This is especially
important for self-completion questionnaires as an
interviewer will not be present to assist if a question does
not make sense.

Market research

Finally, you must be willing to abandon your pre-conceived
ideas if the research does not result in the findings
you expected.

## Marketing budget

Marketing budget

There are no hard and fast rules about how much money
you should invest in marketing. A general rule of thumb
would be to spend between 2 and 10% of your revenue,
depending on how well established you are, your occupancy
levels, and so on.

The most important point is to set an affordable budget and
stick to it. You may find it helpful to divide the budget
according to the various promotional tools and to review this
each month to check you are not exceeding it. This will also
help you to sound more convincing and to say 'no' when
advertising sales people telephone you with one of their
last-minute offers. If the activity is not in a pre-set budget,
then don't do it!

Do remember to include a contingency for additional
marketing in case of a sudden downturn, whether this is
caused by the economy, terrorism or the weather.

Finally, at the end of each financial year, compare the budget
you set with the budget you spent. You might also like to
make adjustments as the internet becomes an even more
prominent source of business.

## Checklist for a marketing action plan

### 1 CURRENT SITUATION

- What is the product or experience you are offering?
- What are the key benefits?
- Who are your current markets?
- What general trends might affect your business, negatively or positively?

### 2 MARKETING OBJECTIVES

- What objectives do you want your marketing plan to achieve?
- How will you know if it has been successful?
- What timescale and deadlines have you set?

### 3 SWOT ANALYSIS

- What are your strengths?
- What are your weaknesses?
- What opportunities do you have?
- What are the threats that you face?
- How can you maximise those strengths and opportunities?
- What can you do to minimise those weaknesses and threats?

### 4 COMPETITOR ANALYSIS

- Who are your competitors?
- What do they offer?
- What are their prices – how do yours compare?
- What are their markets?
- How do they promote themselves?
- What are the relative advantages and disadvantages of their product compared to yours?
- How can you learn from them?
- Are there any opportunities you could exploit which they are missing?

### 5 COMPETITIVE ADVANTAGE/UNIQUE SELLING POINT

- How are you going to compete?
- Do you need to invest more in marketing?
- Do you need to develop new products?

- Can you offer a product or experience which is truly different and better than your competitors?
- Can you focus on the niche markets whose needs you understand and can satisfy?
- What is your Unique Selling Point?

### 6 MARKET RESEARCH

- What market research do you need to undertake?
- When and how often do you need to do it?
- How will you do it?
- What size of sample will you need?
- How do you plan to implement the results?

### 7 TARGET MARKETS

- Which will be your primary markets?
- Which will be your secondary markets?
- Which market segments will you target?
- What do you already know about those markets?
- What do you need to find out?

*For each market segment*

- What is their level of awareness of your product?
- Do you need to adapt your product in any way?
- Do you need to adapt your pricing structure?
- What channels of distribution do they use – how will they access your product or make a booking?
- What channels of communication are most appropriate for that market?
- What promotional messages do they most want to hear?

### 8 PROMOTIONAL TOOLS

For each market segment you will need to select appropriate tools and messages.

- Which tools will you use and how?
  - Brochure and print material?
  - Advertising?
  - PR activities?
  - Direct mail?
  - The internet?
  - Exhibitions?
  - Sales activities?

- Will you be able to work with a consortium?
- How will you work with the tourist boards?
- Will you need to employ consultants to do any of the work?

### 9 MONITORING

- What methods will you use to monitor the effects of your marketing activities?
- When will you do that?
- When will you review your marketing plan and develop a new one?

You have finished developing your marketing plan – but remember it doesn't stop here. Now you have to make sure you implement all the steps you have identified. It is also essential to keep evaluating what you have done, thinking how it could be improved.

You should now be ready to select your target markets and choose and use appropriate promotional tools. The next two chapters will deal with these aspects.

# Chapter 4
# Choosing target markets

This chapter looks at one of the most important elements of marketing – deciding whom you'll target and what they want to hear. If your accommodation accurately matches the needs and perceptions of potential markets, your promotional activities will be made much easier.

We consider how to make sure you really understand your customers and look at some of the latest segmentation techniques. They can help to prevent wasting money on unproductive markets.

## Using segmentation techniques

The total market for tourism products is huge. It is made up of people looking for budget accommodation and rooms in exclusive country house hotels, of sun-worshippers and culture vultures, of couch potatoes and ardent adventurers. You cannot hope to satisfy all of the people all of the time. Nor should you try to target all of them at once. Broadcast marketing or using a 'something for everyone' approach is expensive and rarely successful.

Segmentation means breaking markets down into a more manageable size, and gaining a precise understanding of different groups of people. Once you understand what each group needs and expects, you can then choose which segments you are most likely to satisfy. It is far more productive and cost-effective to identify several smaller groups of people or market segments.

## Six-point plan

The following six-point plan will help you to use segmentation and choose the most productive target markets for you.

### 1 CONSIDER CURRENT MARKETS

If your business is established you should already have a good idea of who your guests are and know something about them. Whether you can do it from memory and the many informal conversations you have had with your guests, or you need to look through your records, make a note of the types of guests you already have.

Don't just think about concrete facts, such as where they come from and their average age; think also about what sort of people they are. What makes them want to come to stay with you? What are their hobbies, interests and passions? The more information you have about your current guests, the easier all future marketing will be.

You can increase profitability simply by focusing on current markets and persuading them to stay longer, visit you more frequently or recommend you to their friends and relatives.

It is almost always easier to attract more guests like the ones you already have, than to tackle completely new markets. Think of your marketing as having a ripple effect, focusing on the bull's eye of your core market and then gradually extending your reach outwards.

### 2 THINK ABOUT THE PRODUCT AND SERVICE YOU OFFER

In Chapter 3 we considered ways to develop a Unique Selling Point. You need to think about that again now.

Marketing is about the relationship between what you are offering and what your customers want. It is only when your product and their perceptions match that they will buy. So it stands to reason that if you can find out more about what makes your current customers 'tick', you will understand more about them. This will enable you to choose images that appeal to them, use the language they feel comfortable with and show that what you offer is exactly what they want.

You might also like to consider your guests' motivations for using your accommodation. Do they respond to special offers and other triggers? Or do they come because you are in an area that they have always wanted to visit? Perhaps they come because they need to – to visit people or on business? Some guests might come again and again, simply because they like it so much and feel secure doing the same thing each year. Is there a particular aspect of your accommodation about which guests often make positive comments?

3  DRAW UP A 'LONG LIST' OF POTENTIAL MARKETS
Try to be as realistic as possible. If, for example, you think your USP is offering peace and relaxation in a very tranquil setting, your accommodation might not be appropriate for families with teenage children.

When choosing market segments you will need to ensure that they are:

- easily identifiable and distinct from the mass market;
- large enough to make targeting them worthwhile – you should also consider whether or not they are growth markets;
- easy to reach, either because they are geographically close to you or there are obvious and established channels of distributions and media through which you can target them.

4  DECIDE WHICH SEGMENTATION METHOD YOU WILL USE
Some of the factors and methods you can choose to use are described below.

*Geographic*
Knowing where potential guests live is a good starting point. It helps to determine catchment areas, distribution channels and routes to market, and is particularly useful for overseas marketing. We cannot target the whole of the world, but we can focus on individual countries. However, we also need to remember that not everyone from one area acts in the same way or has the same likes and motivations.

Six-point plan
- 1 CONSIDER CURRENT MARKETS
- 2 THINK ABOUT THE PRODUCT AND SERVICE YOU OFFER
- 3 DRAW UP A 'LONG LIST' OF POTENTIAL MARKETS
- 4 DECIDE WHICH SEGMENTATION METHOD YOU WILL USE
- 5 DEVELOP AND DESCRIBE THE SEGMENTS
- 6 DOUBLE CHECK YOUR SEGMENTS AGAINST OTHERS'

*Socio-demographic*

Most traditional segmentation methods rely heavily on socio-demographic factors, such as age and income. Whilst these might sometimes offer a good basis and framework, they do not help to create a true picture of target markets.

Using factors such as age and disposable income can be misleading if used on their own. For example, a 50-year-old woman might be down at heel, exhausted by her errant teenage progeny and frustrated by constant trips to Sainsbury's to feed an unappreciative family. She could equally be using her divorce settlement to enjoy a world cruise with her new boyfriend. There is no longer such a thing as 'acting one's age'.

Furthermore, income does not necessarily determine spending, as Britain's enormous credit card and mortgage debt demonstrates.

In theory, teenagers have very limited income compared to, say, professional working adults. However, their disposable income might be considerable, thanks to their 'pester power' and spending money from parents and grandparents. They have few other responsibilities, so they feel more justified in spending over £100 on the latest sports footwear than their parents.

Another difficulty is that many tourism businesses still choose to target similar markets. For example, there is enormous competition for a market defined as 'professional working couples from X region aged 35–55'. This is a very broad market and it is actually hard to imagine what these people are like. If you cannot really imagine a market, it is hard to develop appropriate marketing messages.

*Life stage factors*

The next development in market segmentation is to profile people according to life stage factors, hence tags such as 'DINKYs' (Dual Income, No Kids Yet) or 'empty nesters' when children have left home and the parents are perhaps 'SKI' (Spending their Kids Inheritance) on tourism products.

This method can work better than more traditional methods because it is easier to build up a picture of each segment. Life stage does influence how much people spend, and on what.

However, this only works if we assume that everyone passes through the same family life cycle: child; teenager; adult; one half of a couple; couple with children; empty nester; elderly couple; elderly person living alone. In practice, this does not always happen and does not take account of changing family dynamics.

Life stage is undoubtedly important but should not be taken in isolation. Other factors, such as whom someone is with at the time of making a purchase/decision, are equally important. A married woman with a young family may act like a mother/wife for most of the year, but when she is able to enjoy a weekend with girlfriends, her behaviour and purchasing decisions are likely to be very different. Again, life stage criteria are useful but not in isolation.

*Using psychographic characteristics*

This means considering people's values and emotional reactions and motivations.

Arkenford Ltd have developed the ArkLeisure Model™ which VisitBritain has used to help determine its domestic markets. Some of the considerations were: how each segment feels towards new ideas and trends; how much they demonstrate independence of mind or are influenced by those around them; and accepted norms.

The eight segments are summarised in the following table. The percentage in the final column indicates the potential size of each of these segments in the UK.

| Segment | Description | Segment (%) |
|---|---|---|
| **Style hounds** | • 'Young, free and single'; impulsive. | 11.6% |
| | • Fashion counts. | |
| | • Brand counts. | |
| | • Looking for fun with friends. | |
| | • Most not seriously sporty. | |

*continued*

Six-point plan

- 1 CONSIDER CURRENT MARKETS
- 2 THINK ABOUT THE PRODUCT AND SERVICE YOU OFFER
- 3 DRAW UP A 'LONG LIST' OF POTENTIAL MARKETS
- 4 DECIDE WHICH SEGMENTATION METHOD YOU WILL USE
- 5 DEVELOP AND DESCRIBE THE SEGMENTS
- 6 DOUBLE CHECK YOUR SEGMENTS AGAINST OTHERS'

| Segment | Description | Segment (%) |
|---|---|---|
| Cosmopolitans | • Strong, active, confident.<br>• Style and brand important, but as an expression of their self-made identity.<br>• High spenders especially on innovation and technology.<br>• Looking for new challenges, new experiences; globetrotters. | 15.2% |
| Discoverers | • Independent in mind and action.<br>• Little influenced by style or brand, but interested in new options.<br>• Buy on function and value to them.<br>• Looking for new and educational experiences. | 12.8% |
| High street | • Mainstream early adopters.<br>• Followers of high-street fashion.<br>• Care what others think.<br>• Happy to buy package options. | 21.2% |
| Followers | • Strongly influenced by what others will think.<br>• Don't want to be seen as old-fashioned.<br>• Less active.<br>• Slow to adopt.<br>• Avoid risk. | 10.5% |
| Traditionals | • Self-reliant; internally referenced.<br>• Slow to adopt new options.<br>• Strong orientation towards traditional values.<br>• Value individual attention and service. | 12.4% |
| Habituals | • Largely inactive, low-spending group.<br>• Very traditional; strongly resistant to change.<br>• Risk adverse.<br>• Value relaxation, peace and quiet. | 7.0% |
| Functionals | • Self-reliant.<br>• Price driven.<br>• Value function over style.<br>• Traditional values, but interested in new experiences; not risk adverse. | 9.4% |

This approach is more effective in getting into the minds of potential market segments and therefore being able to develop more persuasive marketing messages.

Segmentation usually involves combining the above methods so you can develop a complete profile for different market segments. The more detail you can add about different segments, the better. The total market for any product is likely to be quite wide, but by describing the differences between segments, it becomes possible to create focused and cost-effective strategies for each one.

It doesn't matter which segmentation method you use, so long as you are able to describe your potential markets in some detail.

5 DEVELOP AND DESCRIBE THE SEGMENTS

You now need to decide which segments could potentially show the most promise for you and start to describe them in more detail. Your first attempt at potential segments will probably be fairly long. Divide the list into primary and secondary targets. It is best to select around four market segments to target. If you select any more than that, your promotional resources will be too stretched.

**Primary targets** will generally correspond to current client groups. These should ideally be segments showing good growth, which are fairly easy to target because you already know a lot about them and have been successful in attracting them.

**Secondary markets** may be more difficult to reach and represent a more long-term objective, but show excellent potential.

If you can describe each segment in some detail you will find it much easier to picture them and write more compelling information for your website and print material. It sometimes helps to prop up a photograph of someone who looks like how you imagine one of your segments to look.

Here are some of the questions you might like to ask in order to develop detailed descriptions of your segments:

Six-point plan
- 1 CONSIDER CURRENT MARKETS
- 2 THINK ABOUT THE PRODUCT AND SERVICE YOU OFFER
- 3 DRAW UP A 'LONG LIST' OF POTENTIAL MARKETS
- 4 DECIDE WHICH SEGMENTATION METHOD YOU WILL USE
- 5 DEVELOP AND DESCRIBE THE SEGMENTS
- 6 DOUBLE CHECK YOUR SEGMENTS AGAINST OTHERS'

- What are the basic essentials about this segment such as age, socio-economic, life stage, etc.?
- What are their interests?
- Are they likely to be travelling on business or for pleasure?
- Who are they likely to be travelling with?
- Why are they with that person/those people? Does it make a difference?
- How do they decide to visit somewhere? Where do they get their information from?
- Are they affected by other people's opinions or more independently minded?
- What motivates them?
- What sort of benefits are they interested in?
- Are they forward-thinking people or do they prefer things to be the way they've always known them?
- What are they likely to tell other people about the area when they go home?
- What are their lasting memories likely to be about?
- What aspects of your accommodation do you think they'll particularly like?
- Is there anything you think they'll be less keen on?

Once you have chosen your segments, you need to be certain that they show enough promise and growth to be worth targeting. They should also be relatively easy to reach.

You might like to use some of the following questions to validate each of your segments. Some people like to answer these questions in full to help them prioritise their markets, whereas others prefer to give the responses a numerical value. Whichever approach you use, you might find that at this stage you want to reject a segment as being too small or difficult, to combine two segments into one or split one segment into two.

Let us take the example of the owner of a small hotel in the Lake District who is thinking of targeting young professional families from the Greater Manchester area. This target market would love to live in the country but need to be close to Manchester for work. Their children are pre-school age and the parents want to make sure they get the best possible start in life. They are quite forward-thinking people but also enjoy the idea of a traditional family environment.

Six-point plan

- 1 CONSIDER CURRENT MARKETS
- 2 THINK ABOUT THE PRODUCT AND SERVICE YOU OFFER
- 3 DRAW UP A 'LONG LIST' OF POTENTIAL MARKETS
- 4 DECIDE WHICH SEGMENTATION METHOD YOU WILL USE
- 5 DEVELOP AND DESCRIBE THE SEGMENTS
- 6 DOUBLE CHECK YOUR SEGMENTS AGAINST OTHERS'

### Segment A – 'Caring Families'
*(You will find it helpful to give each segment a name.)*

| | |
|---|---|
| Segment size | Large and probably growing. |
| Likely length of stay | At least two nights, possibly up to a week. |
| Spend | Medium (they have plenty of demands on their income but value family holidays highly). |
| Disposable time | Good. |
| Seasonal spread | Throughout the year, and can travel outside school holidays. |
| Growth potential | Excellent. |
| Product fit | Very good – so long as the hotel can convince them there is plenty to do in the area and the hotel can offer suitable and healthy food. |
| Likely to repeat visit/ word of mouth | Very high. |
| Cost of reach | Relatively low – could advertise in parent magazines in Greater Manchester area; use word of mouth and PR – especially if the hotel can offer something special for this target segment, such as picnic lunches for children and parents, and directions to five local activity centres suitable for children. |
| Knowledge of segment | Is relatively easy to imagine the needs of this kind of segment, and therefore to be confident that the hotel can meet their needs. |
| Segment's knowledge and awareness of the Lake District | Strong – their families used to take them when they were little and they have continued to return from time to time. |

6 DOUBLE CHECK YOUR SEGMENTS AGAINST OTHERS'

This is a good way of making sure you are spending your marketing budget wisely. Find out which markets other organisations are targeting so you can piggy-back on their efforts and take advantage of their greater marketing spend.

Tourism marketing works with a kind of funnel effect, so that the tourist boards grab the attention of visitors, inform and persuade them to come to Britain/your country/your area.

VisitBritain promotes Britain in international markets and promotes England to the domestic markets. In overseas markets, it divides the market according to geographic origin and looks to some extent at the life stage of potential visitors. In domestic markets it uses the ArkLeisure Model™ which focuses more on values.

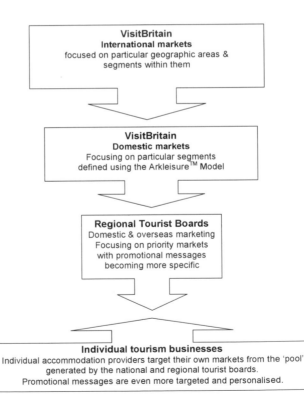

**VisitBritain**
**International markets**
focused on particular geographic areas &
segments within them

**VisitBritain**
**Domestic markets**
Focusing on particular segments
defined using the Arkleisure™ Model

**Regional Tourist Boards**
Domestic & overseas marketing
Focusing on priority markets
with promotional messages
becoming more specific

**Individual tourism businesses**
Individual accommodation providers target their own markets from the 'pool'
generated by the national and regional tourist boards.
Promotional messages are even more targeted and personalised.

If you choose similar segments to them, you will be benefiting from their umbrella marketing and are more likely to get a better return on your investment.

The diagram shows this funnel effect. Tourist boards help to develop new markets and generate new visitors. Accommodation providers and other tourism businesses need to reach out to them with their marketing messages.

It makes sense to look at the markets that VisitBritain targets at home and abroad. You can also obtain the marketing plan from your regional tourist board to make sure you know about their regional priorities.

For example, VisitBritain's domestic marketing focuses on the three specific market segments most likely to take short breaks and be influenced by the 'Enjoy England' message. These are taken from the Arkleisure Model™ and are respectively Cosmopolitans, Discoverers and High streets.

## Reaching specific markets

The list of potential target segments is, of course, huge. You might like to think about some of these markets.

### COUPLES

Accommodation providers often say that they want to target couples, but little thought seems to be given to what kind of couples they are aiming at. Think a little and you are sure to come up with a whole host of different segments. For example, they could be young couples in the first flush of romance or middle-aged couples enjoying 'second time around' relationships. They might be professionals looking for rest and relaxation away from their busy life, or seeking excitement through an active outdoor activity. They could be active retired people enjoying the freedom of their empty nest, or people who have gone away as a reward to themselves or a celebration.

Each of these sets of people will have slightly different needs and may need some additional facilities.

Six-point plan

1 CONSIDER CURRENT MARKETS

2 THINK ABOUT THE PRODUCT AND SERVICE YOU OFFER

3 DRAW UP A 'LONG LIST' OF POTENTIAL MARKETS

4 DECIDE WHICH SEGMENTATION METHOD YOU WILL USE

5 DEVELOP AND DESCRIBE THE SEGMENTS

6 DOUBLE CHECK YOUR SEGMENTS AGAINST OTHERS'

Reaching specific markets

COUPLES

FAMILIES

SINGLE PEOPLE

PETS

VISITS TO FRIENDS AND RELATIVES

BUSINESS TRAVELLERS

### FAMILIES

'Families' is another huge market which is worth breaking down into smaller categories. The needs of a family with young children are very different to those with teenagers. Families may be coming away as part of their usual holiday or perhaps for a family celebration.

As more and more families become spread out throughout the country and no longer all live in the same community, there is a growing trend towards extended families meeting up and going away together.

One of the advantages of families as a target market is that they are often willing to book well in advance in order to secure the rooms they need.

If you can offer family rooms or rooms that are close together suitable for families with young children, make sure you stress this in your promotional materials.

### SINGLE PEOPLE

As life expectation grows and people choose to get married or settle down later in life, there are growing numbers of single people. They may be travelling alone perhaps on business, or come together as a group.

Single travellers have often been treated quite badly by accommodation providers. They may be offered pokey rooms, charged high single room supplements and given the worst table in the restaurant. If there is a way you can provide a better service for people travelling on their own, do make them aware of this. You will be in the minority and can add this to your list of USPs. And remember that not all people travelling alone will always travel alone – next time they may bring their family and friends.

### PETS

Not many accommodation establishments accept pets. If you do choose to welcome pets (and are aware of the disadvantages such as increased cleaning), this can be another USP. There are several guides in which you can advertise or you could generate some free publicity for yourself by offering novel services for the pets themselves, such as welcoming them with a new toy.

### VISITS TO FRIENDS AND RELATIVES

Visits to Friends and Relatives, or 'VFR', is already an important market and one which is growing rapidly. Not all friends and families will want to use paid-for accommodation, but a proportion will, depending on their personal circumstances and reasons why they are travelling.

Some may be attending weddings, christenings or other celebrations in your area, so make sure you make friends with your local wedding and party venues. They may include your accommodation in their list of recommendations.

### BUSINESS TRAVELLERS

It is likely that a proportion of your guests will be travelling on business. Their needs will be slightly different to those of leisure travellers in that they will probably want an earlier breakfast and possibly somewhere they can work. They will almost certainly appreciate wireless internet access if you can provide it.

Remember that so-called business travellers come in many guises. They may be visiting local firms or they could be temporarily working in the area. Contractors such as builders may need somewhere to stay close to their site for several weeks or months. They will probably want early breakfasts but can offer you good regular business all year round.

## Promoting through intermediaries

The travel trade acts as an intermediary between the public and tourism products. Depending on the size of your establishment and your current occupancy levels, you might find it productive to work with the travel trade to generate more business. They will want either discounted rates or commission payments, but in return can offer you exposure to a variety of markets that might otherwise be hard to reach.

This is a very cost-effective marketing method. The travel trade has multiple purchasing power so once you have identified one key decision-maker they can bring numerous visitors, either as individuals or groups.

Some accommodation providers assume that the best way to get more business through the travel trade is to mail travel agents, but this is usually a waste of money because they only make bookings via tour operators. It might, however, be worth identifying some business travel agents who make arrangements for corporate travellers.

Tour operators package the individual components of a holiday or tour, negotiating inclusive fares for travel, accommodation and some sightseeing. As the name implies, short break operators promote accommodation packages for up to four nights. This is a growth market, albeit a competitive one, and short break operators are continually looking for new destinations and activities to package.

They usually demand high commissions (up to 30%) but in return can offer substantial business, sometimes at off-peak times. Take a look at the domestic short break brochures in your local travel agents to find out which short break operators might be worth approaching.

Incoming tour operators can be invaluable in helping you to reach overseas' markets without the expense of overseas' promotion.

There is no point in targeting coach operators and group travel organisers unless you have at least ten bedrooms and are prepared to contract all of them at once, which could jeopardise some of your other regular business.

However, if you do have sufficient rooms (or perhaps a large enough catering room to accommodate them for a coffee or meal stop), they can provide excellent business. Coach operators range from huge operators who publish their own brochures to smaller companies more interested in ad hoc private hire from societies.

## Inside their heads?

Good marketing depends on accurate and appropriate targeting and tailoring messages and promotions to your chosen markets.

Think about the buyer/seller relationship. Who is the most powerful? Most sales people answer 'the buyer' but in fact the buyer and seller have to be absolutely equal and in agreement in order for a sale to take place. The buyer must want the product at the selling price and the seller must want to sell at that moment and at that price. Realising that selling is all about making this relationship more equal somehow makes the process easier and less daunting.

If you can really understand your target market and what is in their mind, you'll find it quite easy to write convincing sales copy, develop better brochures and to sell directly to them. Here are a few tips to help you really get inside the mind of your potential guests.

Choose just one important market segment and go through the questions in 5: Develop and Describe the Segments. You don't need to write an essay – just scribbling down some details will help.

Once you've done that, write down some notes about your key selling points and the features of your accommodation that you're most proud of. You might find it useful to refer back to the information about Unique Selling Points in Chapter 3.

Go through your list of selling points and features but as you do so think about the target market you've described and their likely reaction to each of those points.

If you really think about your target market, you'll realise that some selling points are more important than others. You might want to prioritise them in a different way, and perhaps even to describe them differently.

continued

Promoting through intermediaries

Consider what some of your target markets' concerns might be. What could the possible barriers to booking your accommodation be? Once again, think about these from the perspective of the people you're targeting and try to find ways of overcoming them.

This exercise needn't be particularly formal or take a long time. But if you spend a little time doing it now, you'll find that all of your marketing activities are easier and more effective. You'll probably find yourself writing in a different, more powerful way and being ready to look at your accommodation from the perspective of a potential guest.

Understanding how someone is likely to think makes it much easier to sell to them because you are ready to describe your accommodation in a more appealing way.

Many group travel organisers work on a voluntary basis to arrange trips for their club or association. The advantage of working with all of them is that they book in advance and you deal with just one person in order to secure a block booking.

You can find out more about them by subscribing to publications such as Group Leisure or Group Travel Organiser.

Do bear in mind that it is general practice to offer one free place for the driver/guide or group leader if there are more than about 20 people in a group.

## Customer Relationship Management

There is much hype surrounding Customer Relationship Management, or CRM as it has become more commonly known. It is basically a planned and consistent process for keeping in touch with customers, both before and after they have bought or booked something.

Some larger businesses use complex tracking and database systems in order to plan and control their pre- and post-sales activities, but this is generally not necessary in smaller companies. In practice you can just as easily use your own straightforward database, diary or card index system.

Promoting through intermediaries

Most owner-operated businesses practise CRM, even if they don't realise it! They are generally doing something that comes naturally to them, showing interest in their guests and asking questions that enable them to provide a better service. Hotel owners may greet regulars by name and show them to their favourite room. They may use memory prompts to send birthday cards, or if a guest has mentioned a forthcoming family celebration, they remember to ask about it afterwards.

Customer Relationship Management

CRM is all about really focusing on customers and knowing as much as possible about them, so long as this is not intrusive. It enables you to provide a better service, and to be able to anticipate any problems and handle complaints in a timely and friendly fashion. And perhaps most importantly, it can help you up-sell and be more profitable. This means, for example, that if you know a couple are staying with you in order to go walking, you might offer a picnic lunch, or if you know that they are celebrating something you could recommend a bottle of wine for dinner.

## Further information

Further information

For more details about the ArkLeisure Model™ from Arkenford Ltd **www.arkenford.co.uk**.

VisitBritain's industry website has several sections that provide insight into different markets and market trends. Look for the Market Intelligence and Research and the Visitor's Voice sections on **www.visitbritain.com/ukindustry**.

Contact your Regional Tourist Board (or equivalent) to ask for a copy of their marketing plan and what research they are able to make available to you

# Chapter 5
# Making the most of promotional tools

Promotional activities are probably the best known and loved aspect of marketing. By this we mean the process of communicating with selected target markets, using appropriate messages. This chapter considers how promotional tools work.

The 'menu' of promotional activities is diverse, and includes such activities as promotional print, public relations (PR), advertising, the internet, direct mail and sales activities. This chapter gives advice on choosing each of these tools and making them work for you.

## Choosing the most appropriate promotional tools

The promotional tools you select will essentially be determined by your target markets and marketing budget. On the subject of budgets, it is worth mentioning that few organisations consider their marketing budget to be big enough. It is not unusual for small budgets to be blamed for a lack of success. A bigger budget can make life easier, but it is possible to make an impact without major expense. Small budgets mean marketing efforts are more focused and have to be carefully planned.

Just as you have hopefully spent some time thinking about your marketing plan, it is important to set timescales and plan promotional activities carefully. Whenever possible, you should test promotional ideas before launching them to the wider world, and make sure you build in monitoring methods.

Some of the factors which should influence your choice of promotional tools are:

Choosing appropriate
promotional tools

– 1 TARGET MARKETS

– 2 WHAT YOU ARE
  OFFERING

– 3 YOUR COMPETITORS

– 4 AWARENESS OF
  YOUR
  ACCOMMODATION

### 1 TARGET MARKETS

Which promotional methods are your potential guests used to? Is it better to use the ones that they accept and which experience proves they react to, or perhaps make an impact by trying something different?

Consumer and trade marketing are very different. Consumers need to be given information and messages to make them want to buy. The travel trade need to be given information which inspires them to sell the product to consumers.

### 2 WHAT YOU ARE OFFERING

Some accommodation is more complex than others. Some needs full explanations, so a brief radio advertisement would be inappropriate. It is very difficult to convey atmosphere or ambiance through some media.

### 3 YOUR COMPETITORS

Some activities will be determined by those of your competitors. This is why it pays to be aware of what they are doing. If they undertake a major advertising campaign and it looks like you could lose market share, the only option may be to retaliate with a stronger campaign (but not necessarily more expensive). Or you may decide to focus on different markets and use different promotional activities for more impact.

### 4 AWARENESS OF YOUR ACCOMMODATION

If you have just started up your business, you will need to do more promotion than established accommodation. Advertising and PR activities are likely to reach a larger number of potential customers than face-to-face sales. Conversely, well-established accommodation will need an extra push from time to time, perhaps using direct mail to remind previous guests to return.

## Understanding the purchasing cycle

Understanding the
purchasing cycle

When anyone buys or books anything, they move through five stages. These are: **unawareness**, **awareness**, **understanding**, **conviction** and **response**. Think about this from your own experience and remember a holiday you have perhaps enjoyed in a previously unfamiliar location.

At first you were pretty much *unaware* of it and what it had to offer. You became *aware* of it, maybe by hearing about it from a friend or seeing an article in a magazine. Then you started to find out more and could see what was in it for you – you *understood* what that destination offered and started to feel *convinced* that it matched what you were looking for in a holiday. You then took the most important step and *responded* to all the information and promotional messages about that destination and actually made a booking. Next time you go away you will already be aware of that destination and understand what it has to offer, but you will need to be convinced that it is worth visiting again.

Understanding this cycle helps you to think about your potential markets and to choose the most appropriate promotional tools according to their level of awareness.

## Matching promotional tools and messages to levels of awareness

| Stage | Promotional tools | Messages |
|---|---|---|
| **Unawareness** | Some advertising and PR. If more direct tools like brochures were used at this stage, they would be ineffectual, as the target markets are not ready for detailed information. | Relatively general, positioning messages. At this stage most work is done by the tourist boards, rather than individual accommodation providers. |
| **Awareness** | Advertising, PR and websites. | Promotion is still inspirational and persuasive, encouraging target markets to show a stronger interest and to want to find out more. |

| Stage | Promotional tools | Messages |
|---|---|---|
| Understanding | Advertising, PR, websites and brochures. | Messages now also include more information as well as inspiration, helping target markets to answer the vital question, 'What's in it for me?' |
| Conviction | Advertising, PR, websites, brochures, direct mail and face to face or telephone sales. | Much more detailed and focused, although still persuasive. Information becomes more detailed, answering questions on specifics such as facilities and prices. |
| Response | Similar to conviction stage. | Very focused and specific messages, action-oriented so the only decision left to make is how to book/buy and pay. |

Understanding the purchasing cycle

Matching promotional tools and messages to levels of awareness

## Remember AIDA

Remember AIDA

Another way of thinking about this in practical terms is to remember that all promotional activities need to work through the 'AIDA principle', standing for **Attention**, **Interest**, **Desire** and **Action**. You need to grab *attention*, appeal to the potential guests' self-*interest*, arouse the *desire* to buy or book and then urge them to take *action* and actually make a booking.

## Choosing promotional messages

Choosing promotional messages

– PRICE

– HEALTH

– SOCIAL

– STATUS

The actual promotional message you use will depend on the market you are targeting and the means by which you are approaching them. For example, different messages may be necessary for tour operators, members of the public and tourist information centres. Messages designed for consumers will not always have a positive impact on the travel trade. For the travel trade, magic words like 'commission' or 'profit' are more likely to attract attention than 'relax and enjoy. . .'.

Bear in mind too that you will need different types of messages for each promotional method. You will need a very brief and punchy marketing message for a radio advertisement, but could use a variety of longer, more complex messages if a sales person can actually meet people face-to-face.

It helps to be aware of the reasons why people buy, and to recognise that sometimes they appear to be buying for different reasons to their actual motivations. A good example of this was the traditional way in which cruise holidays were sold. People booking on a cruise said that they did so because they wanted to see the world, but considering how little time they would spend in a port and how much at sea, this was not necessarily the case. Cruise operators actually promoted the idea that cruise holidaymakers would be doing something their neighbours had probably not done yet, and therefore enhanced status was an important part of the persuasion.

Understanding some of the reasons people buy can help you to develop more powerful promotional messages.

### PRICE
We buy to get value for money. We buy because something is cheaper than we had expected and therefore a bargain. Greed is a prime motivator although few of us admit it! Sometimes we buy more expensive products because we believe they will be better than cheaper ones or we like the image they convey.

### HEALTH
Holidays are seen as healthy activities, offering the chance to relax. We buy some products because we think they are good for us.

### SOCIAL
This may be a chance to be together with friends or family, or simply a desire not to get left out. Some products are purchased because it becomes normal to have them, rather than for rational reasons.

STATUS

Some products offer a chance to impress. Others are bought because they make a statement about the purchaser or make the purchaser feel good about themselves.

It is said that more than 85% of all decisions are based on emotion rather than logic.

Remember to use some real examples within your message to make your claims credible. A brief anecdote or an intriguing statement can help to bring a place alive and make it more enticing. It does not have to relate directly to your accommodation itself – your location is equally important.

If you can answer any or all of these questions, your promotional message will exert a strong emotional force.

- What emotions can you evoke when someone hears or reads about your product or service?
- Can you save your guests money, make them money, or make them look like they have money?
- Can you help guests to save time or help them to enjoy their time more?
- Can you offer relaxation or stress relief? Can you make your customers happy? Make them feel healthy?
- Can you make your customers feel proud or help them to achieve something?
- Can you help your guests to look or feel younger? Can you offer romance?

## Copywriting counts

At some stage you will need to write about your accommodation, whether for your website, brochure or perhaps for an entry in a tourist board publication. The best copy is often the shortest. If you have a strong product which photographs well, let pictures tell the story.

Most people feel daunted when they sit in front of a blank sheet of paper. To get started, it is easiest if you simply jot down the points you want to cover as they occur to you. You can then sort them into a logical order before you begin to write. Keep in mind two short words as you write: 'you' and 'why?'

Choosing promotional messages

- PRICE
- HEALTH
- SOCIAL
- STATUS

Copywriting counts

- YOU!
- WHY?
- DON'T FORGET TO THINK 'FAB'

### YOU!

Which word immediately attracts your attention? 'You!' We all instantly identify with 'you' and assume it means *us*. Does your promotional literature tell prospective visitors about your facilities instead of conveying what that means for them? Try to avoid the words 'I' or 'we'. Turn the sentence round to imply 'you'. For example: 'All our bedrooms are individually designed and have en-suite facilities' could be rewritten and made to sound more appealing: 'You'll be able to relax in one of our individually designed bedrooms with a private bathroom.'

### WHY?

Keep in mind the reasons why someone would want to stay in your accommodation. For example, family life today can lack a sense of security and freedom, but on holiday families want a chance to relax and enjoy activities together. 'Do you remember those happy relaxed days playing games with your parents? You can recreate those cosy memories with your own children at. . .' uses nostalgia and the human need for togetherness in order to sell.

Many other products are promoted in ways which do not bear a direct relation to the product itself. Perfume manufacturers do not sell smell – they offer romance. Car manufacturers do not promote a method of transport – they offer excitement or reliability. We can learn a lot from these examples. Accommodation can be sold in many different ways – a refuge, a home from home, a place for romance or a chance to relax and recuperate.

### DON'T FORGET TO THINK 'FAB'

Don't forget the difference between **features**, **advantages** and **benefits**. It is easiest to list the features and physical characteristics of what you offer, but visitors are more interested in the *benefits* to them.

Turn round statements like 'We have four bedrooms at the rear of the hotel. . .' so you indicate the advantages and benefits: 'From the bedrooms at the rear of the hotel you'll have a wonderful view of the beautiful countryside.'

## Case study – Mace Court Hotel

*Developing promotional material to appeal to target markets and selling benefits, not features*

Within the area of Paddington in London, there are countless hotels offering budget accommodation, all competing with each other. The majority of hotels are relatively small, privately owned and correspond to the two-star category. Their facilities are similar, their location is similar and they are all competing for a similar market.

It is difficult for many of these hotels to find a competitive advantage and to stand out from the rest. Hotels in this area have a reputation for budget prices, often with budget service. Service and standards in this type of hotel are improving, but they still have to deal with their former reputation as 'bed factories', working on tight margins. Budget hotels have a reputation for often being unfriendly, sometimes dirty and rarely offering any added value.

Most hotels in this category have a very limited marketing budget and only the simplest brochure or website to promote the hotel with. The Mace Court Hotel's brochure stands way above the competition. The owner recognises the importance of some investment in marketing and it has paid off for him.

A professional designer was engaged, as well as a photographer, who has made sure the small but value-for-money bedrooms are presented in a good light.

Instead of listing facilities as many hotels do, the brochure addresses readers directly and tells them how they will benefit from staying in the Mace Court. It stresses its value for money and goes on to say that means the reader will be able to enjoy their stay in London more, which is easy because the hotel is so centrally located. A simple map shows exactly where

continued

Copywriting counts
– YOU!
– WHY?
– DON'T FORGET TO THINK 'FAB'

the hotel is and how many minutes it takes to reach other key points, such as Oxford Circus and some famous museums.

The place is brought alive by mentioning some of the famous people who lived in or near Paddington. It describes some of the most interesting places to visit in Central London, recognising that most of its guests will be first-time visitors who will spend more time out of the hotel than in it.

The brochure and website use plenty of pictures, maps and illustrations to make their point instead of wordy copy. They stress the friendly service offered by all members of staff and use a bright but warm style to express cleanliness. On the website there is even a photo of the owner in a mob cab and rubber gloves cleaning the toilet to stress the cleanliness of the hotel.

The owner of the Mace Court Hotel uses the literature distribution service offered by their tourist board to distribute their brochures at overseas' exhibitions designed for consumers trying to find out more about holidays in Britain.

Whenever possible, tourist information staff are invited to see the hotel so they can recommend it to others. The owner also personally visits incoming and domestic tour operators to sign contracts with them and develop a good relationship.

The investment in marketing has paid off, with higher than average occupancy levels and slightly higher room rates. The Mace Court Hotel does not offer extraordinary facilities, although it is clean, friendly and value for money. But the hotel stands well above other hotels of a similar standard in the same area by telling potential guests what they want to hear – that they will have an enjoyable visit to London. It sells itself and its friendly service by offering additional information and showing how easy it is to enjoy a stay there.

*The hotel name has been changed.*

## Some general tips

You have already identified your target markets so you can imagine a typical reader. Imagine you are writing for that one person instead of a whole crowd of people. Write in ordinary, everyday English. A good way to check if what you have written sounds stilted is to read it aloud. Try to be yourself and convey some of your personality, so your brochure and website sound and look different to others. There may be lots of other similar accommodation, but there is only one you.

Try to avoid long passages of text. You can make them easier to read by using shorter sentences, shorter paragraphs and cross-headings (words or phrases picked out of the text and highlighted).

The aim of writing information for a brochure or website is to sell, so it is sometimes natural to want to boast. Whatever you do, tell the truth! Don't oversell so that people are disappointed. Do remember though that you can often minimise negatives by making them into a feature. It is amazing how slanting floors can be quaint signs of an ancient building – not one which is falling apart.

There are two phrases which tend to be over-used in tourism terms. These are 'unique' and 'something for everyone'. It could be argued that almost every tourism product is 'unique' in some way. 'Unique' has been used so often it has become fairly meaningless. It is more effective to explain exactly what you mean.

'Something for everyone' assumes that the public are ready to fall in with the general masses and take pot luck. Few of us are so easy to please that we actually like the idea of 'something for everyone'. Most people are more likely to react to a more specific appeal.

## Better brochures

Having a brochure used to be essential. Now the internet is taking over as a major promotional tool, you may decide that you can eventually do without a brochure or that you can

### Copywriting counts

- YOU!
- WHY?
- DON'T FORGET TO THINK 'FAB'

### Some general tips

### Better brochures

- WORKING WITH A DESIGNER
- DESIGN HINTS

print fewer copies or a shorter version. This will depend on the propensity of your target markets to use the internet. Many people still feel they want a tangible piece of paper which contains all the vital information and can be taken with them or shown to others.

Before you begin, think about how your brochures will now be used and distributed. The new postal rates may mean that you want to change the size of your brochures in future. If your brochures are likely to be displayed in a rack of some kind, you will need them to be an appropriate size.

Consider the feeling you want your brochure to convey and the sort of words your clients might like to read. 'Efficient' will attract the attention of business people but 'relax and unwind' will appeal more to mothers of young children.

Most people are ready to invest a certain amount of money in good design and print, but the two aspects that make the most difference to the success of a brochure are the written contents and any photographs. Before you go to a designer, make sure you have invested some time to get the contents right. It will cost a lot less this way and make the designer's job easier.

### WORKING WITH A DESIGNER

Now that desktop publishing packages are so easy to use, it is tempting to try to save some money and do your own design, or get someone in your family to do it. Most of the time though, DIY design looks like DIY design and should be avoided. Professional designers cost money – because they are worth it.

When choosing a designer, try to find someone with whom you will enjoy working. Design should be part of a creative process and you need to be able to express yourself clearly. It helps if you have set your budget and any restrictions before you start speaking to designers and printers.

Give your designer as much background information as possible about what you are trying to do. Anything is useful because it helps the designer get a 'feel' for the way you wish to present your product. At this stage, advise of any corporate styles already set. Always provide logos and examples of any previous publicity material. It is useful to give the designer some examples of things you do and do not like so they can visibly gauge what you are looking for. It is also worth gathering together a selection of your competitors' brochures so you can ensure yours is different.

*Design timetable*

Set a schedule for work to be undertaken and bear in mind that producing a brochure can be a long process. Designers and printers can work to very tight deadlines, but an ideal timetable would be:

Week 1:     Brief designer and ask them to develop some initial rough ideas.

Week 3:     Meet to look at roughs and ideas, leaving the designer to develop one idea to full visuals.

Week 4:     Visual produced, including colour swatches and using actual copy – this is effectively the first proof stage and the point after which corrections begin to incur costs.

Week 5:     Return corrections to designer and sign off the final proof.

Week 6:     The designer sends the artwork to the printer.

Week 7:     Final proofs are sent from the printer and you sign them off or make final corrections (charges will be imposed for changes at this stage).

Weeks 8–9: Brochure delivery – print time will depend on quantity to be produced, number of colours and type of finishing.

## DESIGN HINTS

It is usually best to keep the design simple. Complicated designs can be confusing and expensive to print. Don't sacrifice clarity and readability for the sake of 'interesting design'. It is easier to read text in dark colours than light ones. Beware of choosing colours and a style which *you* like, rather than ones which appeal to your target reader.

Check type matter carefully and watch out for simple spelling errors. Author's corrections made at proof stage are charged extra and can be expensive. Make sure that all information is correct and descriptions fair and accurate. Ensure that you have permission to use any borrowed photographs or illustrations. Caption the photographs.

Keep your original artwork in case you need it to form the basis of a new design.

## Photography

Good photography is an essential part of all brochures (and websites). Digital cameras make it easy for almost anyone to take their own photographs, but investing in good professional photography can still make a difference because they will use different lenses, lighting and have much more experience. They also lend a professional eye and can help you to see your accommodation in a fresh light. Remember the following points when selecting or commissioning photographs:

- Decide in advance what you will need to photograph and ensure everything is prepared before the photographer arrives. Don't be afraid of asking if you can look through the camera lens to see if particular photographs will include the things you want in the shot.
- Use captions on pictures, rather than labels. A bedroom is obviously a bedroom and does not need labelling as such, but a caption along the lines of 'treat yourself to a rest' is more compelling.
- Try to show people having fun or carrying out appropriate activities in the photographs, but do not use people for the sake of it – a photograph of an attractive hotel bedroom is more likely to sell than one of the receptionist grinning as she lifts a phone.
- Avoid anything which will date the photographs, such as very fashionable clothes.
- Take a look at the resulting photographs and place a piece of paper over one or two edges. If you cropped the photograph in some way, could you give it more impact? A typical example of this is an exterior shot which shows all the tarmac in front of a guesthouse, with the front door somewhere in the distance. A close-up shot would

work much better. Consider how you make the photograph more attractive. If there are any double yellow lines on the road, these should always be cropped. Doors and gates that are slightly open tend to be more welcoming and appealing than closed ones.

## Working with printers

If you have not worked with printers before, the details can be bewildering. It is often worthwhile asking your designer to manage the whole process for you. They will usually be able to negotiate good rates with printers and ensure that the final print looks exactly how they designed it to look. Designers also understand the print process and are less likely to be confused by the amazing array of printers' terms.

You will need to choose a size for promotional print which is appropriate for your purposes, but also ensure it is easy to distribute, so that it fits brochure display stands or standard envelopes. Unusual size leaflets (such as square ones) grab attention but are expensive to produce and distribute. The paper has to be specially cut and cannot be sent out in standard-sized envelopes.

The most expensive part of printing is preparation – the colour reproduction and machine make-ready. It is cheaper to print extra copies on a long run than to reprint. Work out your print runs carefully – don't just grab a round figure out of the air. You might not need to print as many brochures as previously. Make sure you budget for distribution costs.

The weight of the paper, or what most people think of as the thickness, is an important consideration. Lighter paper is slightly cheaper, but colour can 'bleed' through so the quality suffers.

Make sure that you get a print quote in writing and bear in mind that paper prices can fluctuate quite considerably, so the quote could go out of date if you do not use it fairly soon.

The final stage of print is called finishing, and includes folding, trimming and stitching, or stapling. You will need

to include any special instructions in your brief for
the printer.

### ASKING FOR A PRINT QUOTE

Beware of choosing the cheapest printer you can find. You
will probably find significant differences in cost, but the very
cheapest is unlikely to be the best. Whatever price you are
quoted, you will probably need to add 10% on to the price,
to take account of any changes and unexpected problems.
There is nearly always some unexpected change or cost. Use
the following as a checklist of essential information for your
printer when asking for a quote:

- Quantity required (most people also ask for a 'run-on'
  quote per 1,000 or 10,000).
- Size of finished brochure, and type/weight of paper to
  be used. Will the cover require a different weight paper?
  Most printers will provide samples.
- Number of colours.
- Printed on one or both sides? How many pages?
- Are proofs required?
- How the origination material will be provided (ask your
  designer) – disk type, number of artworks, pictures,
  illustrations, transparencies, etc.
- Any additional requirements, such as folding and
  finishing.
- Deadline for final delivery.

## Effective advertising

Advertising allows you to promote a specific message to a
wide audience – for a fee. It can be an extremely expensive
promotional tool which is notoriously difficult to evaluate.
Hence the famous quote: 'I think half of my advertising is a
waste of time – I just don't know which half'.

Advertising is good for creating and building 'awareness' but
this is not necessarily the same as building sales. There are
few organisations who cannot benefit in some way from an
advertising campaign, but to avoid wasted effort and
expense, it must be even more carefully planned than any
other promotional activity.

## SETTING OBJECTIVES

You might be aiming to develop a new market, and create awareness (and potentially bookings) among guests who have never stayed with you, or you may want to encourage previous guests to use your accommodation again, or to try another aspect of it.

Advertising usually has either strategic or tactical objectives. Strategic advertising is concerned with creating awareness and building an image. It usually takes a more long-term view. Tactical advertising is aimed at specific market segments and persuading them to go to a particular place or buy a certain service, sometimes at a particular time. Tactical advertising takes a more short- to medium-term view.

## CREATING THE RIGHT MESSAGE

Most advertising works best with just one key message. This is especially important if you can only afford to buy a few lines or small space. Faced with a small budget, many accommodation providers react by trying to get the best possible value for money. They cram the space with descriptions and detail so the overriding feeling is one of confusion or crowding.

Circulation figures are important but you need to also consider the probability of converting enquiries to bookings. For example, a small classified advertisement in a national newspaper would be seen by more people than an advertisement in a local destination guide. However, if the destination guide is sent out on request to people who are already interested in your area, the chances of converting enquiries to bookings may be higher. There are no fixed rules to advertising. It might take some experimentation for you to work out which publications work best for you. You might for example decide it is better to place numerous small advertisements in several different regional newspapers and special interest magazines or to invest in just one or two larger advertisements in a handful of carefully chosen guides. The only way you will know what works and what doesn't is by monitoring your enquiries and bookings.

Choosing one main message will help to give even the smallest company a stronger identity. This comes back once again to selling benefits rather than features, and stressing Unique Selling Points.

Use just one strong selling point. This could be something unusual, something intriguing, an accolade, or a fantastic photo. The idea is to use the strong selling point and persuade readers to call for a brochure, book or go to a website for more information. Then you can tell them more and make the booking.

### SELECTION OF MEDIA

However much you plan your advertising in advance, there will always be occasions when an advertising sales person telephones you with a 'special offer'. Some of these might be genuine. Most are not. You should do your best to resist – there will always be another opportunity. Your advertising will be much more effective if it is proactive and planned rather than reliant on those last-minute special offers, especially if they are for new publications which no one has heard of and which disappear almost instantly.

Before booking any space or time, telephone the advertising departments of the media you are interested in and ask for a copy of their media pack. This outlines the various advertising opportunities, costs, and profile of readers, viewers or listeners, as well as giving technical data for the publication or programme.

The choice of publications in which to advertise is vast. In addition to local and national press, there are also special interest magazines and tourist board guides. If you run any special interest holidays or even have a product which could be adapted for special interest holidays, these magazines are very useful. The tourist boards publish numerous guides and brochures. Advertising in these is usually reasonably priced.

When you have obtained media packs and information about relevant publications, use the following criteria to draw up a short list:

### Profile of readership

Do the readers correspond to your target markets? The readership profile should detail readers in terms of age and socio-economic profile, as well as giving further details about hobbies and interests, and any research about holiday-taking habits. Tourism products are a major source of revenue for many publications, so they will usually have more detailed information available if you ask for it.

### Readership

Most publications will give their circulation and readership figures. The readership figures are more interesting because these show the actual number of people who will see and read the publication, not just buy it. For some publications there will be a big difference between the circulation and readership figures. Some of the more upmarket monthly magazines have relatively low circulation figures but a long shelf life and high readership figures – particularly when they are the types of publication you see in doctors' and dentists' surgeries!

When considering readership figures, look also at the distribution method for the publication. Is it one which people really demand, by buying it at a newsagents or requesting it from a tourist information centre? Or one which arrives unrequested through the letterbox?

### Publication date

You will need to plan ahead and choose publications whose copy dates you can meet. Even more important are publication dates. If most people plan and book their holiday with you in November, there is little point advertising in a publication which appears in May, unless it is tactical advertising and you are looking for top-up business.

The media pack will probably include details of forthcoming features which might be relevant to you. Sometimes it is a good idea to advertise within a relevant feature, but remember that competitors will probably be doing the same. It can be useful to stand alone and make a bigger impact at another time, if the timing is right for you.

Effective advertising

- SETTING OBJECTIVES
- CREATING THE RIGHT MESSAGE
- SELECTION OF MEDIA
- EVALUATING ADVERTISING CAMPAIGNS

*Advertising rates*

The deciding factor will inevitably be whether or not you can afford to advertise in your chosen publications and if it is cost-effective. Set your budget in advance and stick to it. You might decide to place your advertising through an agency which should not actually cost you anything because they will take a commission from the publications, and may already have special rates.

Whether you book through an agency or place advertisements direct, always try to negotiate a discount. This may be a first-timers' discount, series discount or just because your advertising budget is too small. Regard advertising rate cards as guidelines only. You can negotiate discounts of as much as 50%. When placing advertisements, always ask if there is any chance of editorial coverage and the name of the person you should contact.

### EVALUATING ADVERTISING CAMPAIGNS

You will never find out which half of your advertising budget was a good investment unless you monitor it. Keep a record of the media in which you advertised, when and the cost. Make sure that all staff are aware of the need to monitor advertising expenditure and ask them to make a point of asking people who book with you where they heard about you, and to make a note of this.

You can also monitor which publications work for you by using different types of advertisement, such as specific packages or codes when people are asked to complete tear-off vouchers for further information.

You will be able to increase the effectiveness of any advertising if it is carefully thought through and planned in advance. You will raise more awareness of your product if advertising coincides with a PR and direct mail campaign.

## Direct mail

Sometimes known as 'junk mail', direct mail does not always have the best press. This is mainly due to the vast number of badly written, untargeted letters which are churned out. But when it is done well, direct mail is a successful and cost-effective promotional tool. Good direct mail is about sending precise sales messages directly to potential or existing customers in their home or office. Similar results can be achieved using E-mail and faxes, but letters are now more of a novelty than E-mails, and spam filters do not get in the way.

Direct mail has many advantages. It addresses individuals by name so it can be highly targeted. You can buy or develop mailing lists and select targets by their job, postcode, income level or interests.

Direct mail is extremely flexible. It is often assumed that mail-shots have to be to huge numbers of people, but they could equally be to just a dozen. You can also experiment, by sending out different types of letters to different targets, to see which is most productive.

Monitoring direct mail is also easier than most promotional methods. You will know exactly to whom you have written so you can assess responses very accurately.

Response rates of around 1% for mailing lists which you have hired and rates of up to 7% for previous customers may sound very low. However, the actual cost of reaching those people is also low compared to other promotional activities. Response rates can be increased using a carefully researched list, good letter and offer, and mechanisms such as response-paid reply cards which make responding easier.

### DEVELOPING MAILING LISTS

Good lists give good results. You will need to either buy a mailing list or develop one yourself. Whichever you choose, ensure it is an absolute maximum of two years old. People's personal circumstances can change enormously and after two to three years there is a good chance they will have either moved, changed job or no longer be interested.

You should think just as carefully about target markets and segments for direct mail as for any other form of promotion. Direct mail is not particularly good for general awareness raising. It works best in markets which are already quite well informed about your product or similar ones.

---

**Effective advertising**

- SETTING OBJECTIVES
- CREATING THE RIGHT MESSAGE
- SELECTION OF MEDIA
- EVALUATING ADVERTISING CAMPAIGNS

---

**Direct mail**

- DEVELOPING MAILING LISTS
- DEVELOPING A SALES PROPOSITION OR OFFER
- WRITING SUCCESSFUL DIRECT MAIL LETTERS
- GENERAL COPY-WRITING TIPS FOR DIRECT MAIL LETTERS
- BUDGETING FOR DIRECT MAIL
- MONITORING YOUR DIRECT MAIL CAMPAIGN

There are numerous list brokers who sell lists which can be divided by geographic region, profession, interest, age and so on. They usually have a minimum order of about 1,000 names, which generally cost around £75–£100 per 1,000. These types of lists may be particularly good if you wish to promote special interest holidays or have identified a particular profession as having strong potential for your product.

The Royal Mail is a useful source of information and free advice about direct mail and will often recommend good mailing houses and brokers.

If you keep your mailing list on computer, bear in mind that under the Data Protection Act you must register your lists and adhere to the conditions of the Act.

You can obtain further information by telephoning the Data Protection Registrar on 01625 545745 or see **www.informationcommissioner.gov.uk**.

Before you conduct a massive mailing, it is worth testing your mailing list and letter by sending it to only a limited number of addresses. If you do not get a response you will either need to improve the list or letter.

### DEVELOPING A SALES PROPOSITION OR OFFER

Direct mail letters are effectively sales presentations on paper. To grab attention and elicit a positive response you will need to make a strong offer. Offers which work are not necessarily discounts. Added value offers convey a more positive message and will probably cost you less. For example, if you are promoting winter short breaks for walkers, you could include a free flask which will be filled with a hot drink each morning before they go on their way, or perhaps a free guide to local walks.

Try to see your product from your customer's perspective and show them a solution to their problems or promise something you know they want, and you can deliver.

### WRITING SUCCESSFUL DIRECT MAIL LETTERS

You will find writing direct mail letters easier and more effective if you follow these key steps:

1  Use a hook to grab attention. This could be an intriguing headline or a question to which the answer is almost certainly 'yes'. For example, if you are a hotel offering short breaks for couples you might start with, 'Would you like to put an extra touch of romance in your life?'

2  The second part of your letter should give some further information which reinforces your earlier question or headline, and gives the details of your 'offer'. The second paragraph or sentence should follow on naturally from the first so the reader is encouraged to continue reading. Don't include too much information at this stage – a couple of sentences will do.

3  At this point many readers will have become cynical and either started to think the offer is too good to be true or there is some catch. You will need to offer reassurance or a further explanation, followed with more information about the offer. If you offer the reassurance at this point, readers will be more inclined to believe what follows.

4  Offer some further information and full details.

5  The final section should push the reader to take action. This could be by using a response-paid coupon, tear-off slip, voucher or simply stating a telephone number or website for bookings. Giving a deadline for action is also effective.

The first impression created by the envelope in which you send your letter is important. Brown paper envelopes are marginally cheaper than white or coloured ones but they look cheap. Window envelopes remind people of bills so although they are practical, they can be off-putting. It is a good idea to check what is printed on your franking machine if you have one and investigate the possibility of changing its message to something which relates to the mail shot.

GENERAL COPY-WRITING TIPS FOR DIRECT MAIL LETTERS
Using these tips will help you to write better direct mail letters:

•  Make sure you start with the target's name. If you do not have one, use another relevant name such as 'Dear walker' or 'Dear worn-out city dweller' instead of Dear Sir or Madam.

- Use a warm, friendly style. Remember to keep a picture of a typical reader in your mind so you write a personalised letter rather than one which is aimed at 2,000 people.
- Read your letter aloud to make sure it does not sound stilted.
- Try to keep your letter to one side of A4 – if it looks longer, recipients may be put off reading it.
- A PS at the end of the letter will usually attract attention, particularly if it reinforces the sales message.
- Use techniques such as underlining or emboldening to stress important elements of the letter. CAPITAL LETTERS ARE MORE DIFFICULT TO READ.
- Make sure you include a deadline for response. If you give an incentive such as '10% discount if you book before December', you will also increase response rates.
- Remember to make your sales letter customer-oriented. Use 'you' rather than 'I' or 'we'.

You can test out response rates by changing different elements of the letter. For example, in one batch of letters you could change your headline or opening sentence. In another you could change the offer you make to see if this makes a difference to response levels. Before you send out your letter, test it on colleagues or even existing customers, and ask them what their response would be or how it could be improved.

### BUDGETING FOR DIRECT MAIL

Do not fall into the trap of only working out how much postage will cost for your direct mail campaign. You will need to take into consideration the list purchase or cleaning, stationery, labels, postage, and envelope-stuffing time. The Royal Mail will provide discounted postage rates on large scale mailings if your mail shot is pre-sorted by post code. For further details speak to your local Royal Mail office.

### MONITORING YOUR DIRECT MAIL CAMPAIGN

You will already know how much your campaign has cost and how many people you wrote to. You will need to make a daily note of responses, and whether they were converted from enquiries into bookings. If you work out the total value of the business generated you will be able to calculate the financial return on your direct mail campaign.

Alternatively, you may decide that the rewards are greater than just direct financial ones, having introduced new customers to your organisation who may return more than once and pass on positive word-of-mouth recommendations to other people.

If you are disappointed by the results of your direct mail campaign, don't give up. Direct mail is a useful medium and it works well for many businesses. You probably need to take another look at your mailing lists, letters or the offer.

Finally, don't just look at your own organisation for inspiration. Start to collect examples of direct mail which you receive and analyse which parts of it you think are successful and why, so you can copy some of the better ideas.

## Public relations

Public relations' activities (PR) are about directing carefully selected messages to key target groups. Effective PR can influence a vast range of different groups of people, encouraging them to come to stay with you. It costs less than advertising, but the downside is that you will have little control over whether or not your efforts are successful because you are not paying for coverage or people's opinions.

Not all PR activities relate to dealing with the media. For example, you might decide to hold open days and invite the press, members of the public or travel trade to see the facilities which you offer.

PR is a very useful PR tool as it relies more on resourcefulness and persistence than financial resources. It can help you to reach a very wide audience and generate media coverage which is viewed much more positively than advertising. Coverage is often perceived as an endorsement of your service. Information that is published as a result of PR activities appears impartial, whereas advertising is often treated with suspicion.

However, you do need to be aware of the disadvantages. Around 90% of all press releases are simply thrown in the bin. You are unlikely to know whether your press release has been used by all the media you have sent it to. Most editors will make a decision whether to publish or not, without contacting you. Press releases are rarely published in their entirety. Most of the time, the first paragraphs are the main ones to be reproduced. This might mean that information is misinterpreted.

### PLANNING PR ACTIVITIES

One of the most frequent reasons for rejection of a press release is because it arrives at the wrong time. Good timing is critical to the success of many PR activities so you need to timetable them in advance. Your timetable should take into consideration the times when people make decisions to book or come to your area, and highlight any times when you will be looking for extra business, as well as including the dates of any special events when you might have a special promotion such as Mother's Day.

You will need to work out which publication or programme dates might be relevant for each date or promotion, and when they need information from you. Bear in mind lead times, which may be a month in advance for weekly publications and up to three or four months in advance for monthly publications. That means that the March edition of the magazine you wish to be featured in could well be planned before Christmas. You will need to take all these factors into consideration in your PR timetable and list the media you plan to approach and different types of story for each date.

If you wish to target daily papers, remember that papers particularly welcome information which reaches them on Monday morning, when other news is thin on the ground. They are also more likely to publish information in July and August when political news items are less frequent.

### CHOOSING SUITABLE MEDIA

Identify the programmes your target markets watch and media they are likely to read, and develop a contact list.

There are several professional directories available which give details of media contacts for trade and consumer press or broadcast media. They can appear quite expensive but save a lot of work, particularly if you need to target specialist media which might be difficult to find.

It is a good idea to take a look at the targeted publications so you can give an appropriate slant to your story.

### WRITING PRESS RELEASES

There are accepted rules for writing press releases which are useful to follow. Of course there are times when you will make a bigger impact by using alternative methods or creating a splash through less orthodox practices, but if you are just beginning to use PR it might be safer to follow the rules. Journalists are not afraid of ridiculing PR activities which go wrong!

Don't use complicated language – try to write in a similar tone to the publications or media you are targeting. Your press release will stand a better chance of being used if the journalist's work is minimal. Try to limit your press release to one side of A4, preferably typed using double spacing and wide margins so the copy is easy for journalists to edit. Write 'press release' at the top of the page and then use a short and punchy headline to grab attention. You need to try to make this sound like it really is news, but don't bother trying to write a clever headline – that is the journalist's job.

Most journalists will decide whether they are going to feature your story by scanning the first sentence, possibly the first paragraph. You do not have long to impress them, so make the point of the story clear in the first paragraph. Try to encompass the essence of the story in the first sentence to entice the reader to continue reading. You should also try to answer the questions 'who?', 'why?', 'what?', 'how?', 'when?' and 'where?'

Your release should be written in the third person, without using 'I' or 'we'. It needs to be factual, objective and informative and not read like it is 'hard-sell' full of PR puff. Remember that most press releases are edited 'bottom up'.

This means that the last part of the release is the most likely to be chopped, so don't put important information there – it should be in the first paragraph.

Most times journalists will not bother to call you, but just in case they need to, make it easy for them to react by putting your contact name, address, telephone numbers and E-mail address at the end of the release. A good tip is to read through the information you have written. If a likely reaction to the release could be 'so what?' you will need to either rewrite the story or consider another angle.

### PRESS PHOTOGRAPHY

Just as with brochures, good photography can really help to make your story more interesting. You might succeed in getting a newspaper photographer if you set up a photo opportunity and phone the news or picture desk in advance. However, if another more newsworthy event happens at the same time you will have missed your chance.

If you use your own photographer you will have the photographs for future use and be able to send them to several publications at once. If you are going to create a photo opportunity think carefully about the type of picture which is most likely to attract attention in your target markets. The best photographs usually show something about to happen, happening or just happened.

You might have to set up the shot and it may look a little contrived. These types of photographs can still be successful if they are imaginative. Think carefully about ways of making your photographs newsworthy. If they include famous people, cute animals or children this is relatively easy. Otherwise you might need to consider an unusual angle, look behind the scenes, intriguing setting or just a good caption.

### INVITING A JOURNALIST TO EXPERIENCE YOUR PRODUCT

One way to get your property featured in the media is to invite journalists to stay with you free of charge. Some members of the media will only write about places where they have stayed themselves.

Do some research to find the right journalists and media. You will need to study appropriate magazines and newsletters or listen to radio programmes and so on in advance to make sure their angles fit what you have to offer. Then you can send an invitation to the journalist, together with information on what you are offering. Journalists will want some sort of story, special angle, news or perhaps a local character to interview as well. Make sure you highlight your Unique Selling Points so it is crystal clear why they should come to stay with you instead of somewhere else.

If they do agree to come to stay with you, make sure you offer a good room but do not treat them too differently from other guests. Don't offer additional services that are not available to 'normal' guests, otherwise they may write something which is not really true about your accommodation. Do be confident though that you have got all the details right before you invite anyone. Don't be over-keen and fawning – the journalist is there to see your product as it is and will not want to be treated with kid gloves.

Journalists are busy people and receive many invitations. You might entice them by inviting them to bring a partner with them so they have someone to enjoy the place with.

It could take some time before any resulting article appears so you might need to be patient. If the article is published (and assuming it is positive!), ask for permission to reproduce it on your website and elsewhere so other potential guests can see it.

### A FEW DO'S AND DON'TS FOR DEALING WITH THE MEDIA

- Recognise that journalists are working to strict deadlines, so make sure you offer accurate and timely information. Try to have everything on hand ready for an enquiry – any facts and figures, photographs, etc.
- Don't hassle journalists by telephone. It is hard for them to do their writing job if they keep getting telephone interruptions. You can probably trust that the post has delivered your release so you don't need to call to ask if they have received it, although you might like to ask if there is any further information or material they need.

**Public relations**

- PLANNING PR ACTIVITIES
- CHOOSING SUITABLE MEDIA
- WRITING PRESS RELEASES
- PRESS PHOTOGRAPHY
- INVITING A JOURNALIST TO EXPERIENCE YOUR PRODUCT
- A FEW DO'S AND DON'TS FOR DEALING WITH THE MEDIA
- ADVERTORIALS
- COMPETITIONS AND PRIZES
- OVERSEAS' PRESS

- Remember that journalists are not always in control of the final article that gets published. Their editor may decide there is not enough space or a bigger story may push yours out of the paper. It is pointless complaining to the journalist, even if you felt you have invested a lot of time in trying to help them.
- Don't be scared or daunted by journalists. They are ordinary people doing an interesting job. They don't want to be negative or catch you out in some way. In general, they just want to find the easiest way possible of doing their job so if you can help them, they are more likely to feature you.

### ADVERTORIALS

Advertorials are a combination of advertisement and editorial. They usually appear as special features in newspapers or magazines and look like ordinary features but are actually promotional stories paid for by your business and others like it. It normally says something like 'promotional feature' above it so people know you have paid for this space. These advertorials have the benefit of appearing to come from the publication and being in the main body, so they often generate a better response than other advertising even though you may need to pay more.

### COMPETITIONS AND PRIZES

Local and regional papers and commercial radio stations are particularly keen on reader or listener competitions. You could consider giving away a weekend in your accommodation as a prize if they run a competition in their publication or radio programme, and you will benefit from the free publicity.

### OVERSEAS' PRESS

If you are trying to attract overseas' visitors, developing contacts with overseas' press should be an integral part of your plan. VisitBritain invites considerable numbers of journalists to Britain every year so they can experience facilities at first hand. If you are willing to host such visits, you should get in touch with your regional or area tourist board and directly with the VisitBritain press office. More information about working with overseas' press is given in Chapter 8.

## Sales activities

Face-to-face selling is one of the best ways of promoting any product. Because it is so personalised, the sales presentation can be adapted to suit the audience and people are far more persuasive than paper promotions. Selling means actually taking an order or booking, so sales activities are relatively easy to monitor.

Personal sales are very effective, but they must be planned and targeted like any other promotion. The good news is that almost anyone can develop sales skills.

### DEVELOPING SALES SKILLS

A good sales person is not just good at selling. They need to have sound product knowledge, both of your own accommodation and competitors'. The more information and knowledge you have, the more confident you are likely to sound.

You can find sales leads by visiting exhibitions and reading the trade and consumer press. Depending on the size and type of accommodation, you may want to make appointments to visit local companies to encourage them to make bookings with you for any visitors to their company, or to tour operators to encourage them to feature you in their programmes.

### MAKING APPOINTMENTS

The first time you telephone someone in order to make an appointment with them can be daunting. You will feel more confident if you have jotted down what you plan to say to them and thought about the benefits you want to present. Don't launch into a full sales spiel when you telephone someone. Your aim should be to get them to spare a few minutes for you to see them, when you will be able to present your product much more effectively than on the telephone.

You will need to make sure that you see someone who has responsibility for booking or selecting new products. Within tour operators this is usually the role of the contracts manager, but in smaller companies people are less likely to have titles. Find out relevant contact names in advance. If you do not have them, telephone and ask who is responsible for contracting or marketing, then try to make an appointment with them.

If you feel that a secretary is blocking your call, don't leave your number and ask them to ring back. They probably won't. Ask the secretary when the best time to call is and call back then.

You will find it easier to make appointments if you have a concrete reason for the sales meeting, for example, if you have launched a new service or package, or perhaps got some special rates for tour operators.

Be proactive and suggest a time to meet. By suggesting a time like 'quarter to three' you will sound like you are organised and busy and you only have a limited amount of time which will reassure the person you are trying to meet. It is useful to say that you think the meeting will only take about half an hour so it does not sound like you will waste their time. If you have given a time limit for the sales meeting, make sure you stick to it.

Some people will ask you to send them information rather than going to see them. If all else fails and you really do not think they are very interested, then do this. However, it is much better to tell them you need to find out more information about their business so you can give them relevant information and rates.

### PLANNING THE SALES MEETING

Don't just take along a handful of brochures and photographs and turn up at the sales meeting. Plan it so you can really get something out of it, even if it is information instead of a sale.

*Before you go to the meeting*

Think what you already know about the potential client. What can you find out about them? Consider what they need and how you can satisfy that need. You will have to tailor your sales presentation to suit different types of client. For example, a mainstream tour operator may wish to know that you can handle large groups efficiently, whereas someone booking educational travel may be more concerned about safety and educational value.

Make sure you have defined your Unique Selling Point and developed a list of real benefits for that client. Consider what those benefits will mean to your potential client and the best way of presenting them.

Think about the possible objections that the client might raise, and consider how you can overcome them. Doing this in advance will help to build your own confidence, as well as making it more likely that you will get the bookings.

*Thinking about objections*

You will not be able to foresee or overcome all objections. However, you can think about some of them in advance and decide how you will handle them. This way you will be more confident and ready to deal with any objections.

Here are some common objections or delaying tactics and how to deal with them:

| | |
|---|---|
| 'I need to speak to Mr X before I can make a decision.' | Ask when they will be speaking to Mr X and say you will call them shortly after. Or ask if you can speak to Mr X directly. |
| 'I'm not sure' or 'I don't know.' | The client is not raising a tangible objection. They are just not sure and need convincing – continue to sell to them. |
| 'The price is too high.' | Don't start to negotiate a lower price straight away. Try to explain why the price is as high as it is. Don't apologise because this means you also think the price is expensive. This might be a real objection or it could just be part of their usual negotiating tactic. Try to reinforce the reasons why your accommodation is good and worth that price before you agree to reduce prices. Or reduce the price in return for a guaranteed level of bookings.

Another way is to offer to let the client try your product for themselves, because you're sure they will then appreciate that it is really good value for money. |

Sales activities

– DEVELOPING SALES SKILLS
– MAKING APPOINTMENTS
– PLANNING THE SALES MEETING
– AT THE SALES MEETING
– RECOGNISING BUYING SIGNALS

If the client raises several objections during the course of your meeting, it could be that they are really not interested in what you are selling. It could also mean that this is just part of their usual technique. You will probably find that some of the objections are gestures rather than real objections.

Try to analyse and prioritise the objections, rather than locking yourself into a discussion of all of them. Make sure you put any problems into perspective. You can even turn the objection round by asking how you could help the client solve the problem or overcome the objection.

Make sure you stress the advantages and benefits once again so the disadvantages are minimised.

### AT THE SALES MEETING

Don't go into the sales meeting and give a quick run through the wonders of your accommodation. Plan and structure the meeting so you are in control.

It is easy to start a sales meeting with a grumble about the weather or traffic. This is supposed to break the ice, but presents a negative message right from the start. Another bad opening line is, 'I was just passing so I thought I'd come to see you.' This conveys the impression that you do not attribute much importance or priority to the client.

Start with a simple friendly greeting and thank the client for sparing their time to see you. Reassure them that you will not take up more than X minutes of their time. They will think you are business-like and they can relax and focus on what you have to say.

You need to have their full attention. Make an initial sales statement so they will want to listen to you, before you go on to ask questions about their business. For example, 'I think you'll be interested in our new package for tour operators like yourself – but first I just need to ask a few questions to make sure I'm selling you the right product.'

Bear in mind that most potential buyers will be thinking 'What's in it for me?' You will have their attention if you imply you can offer them something of direct benefit. They do not like time-wasters so make sure the sales meeting is structured and directed. This is your opportunity to find out more about the client's business and their needs so you can angle your sales presentation appropriately.

You should have prepared your sales presentation earlier, but don't let it sound like a scripted presentation which you have delivered ten times already that week. Make sure you vary your voice and tone, and ensure you focus on the benefits your product can offer. People buy people, so try to be human and maintain eye contact.

Visual aids such as photographs will help the client to focus on what you are saying and to imagine your product if they are not already familiar with it.

If you use the sort of flip-over table-top presenter which has photographs or sales points for the client to see, you might find it helpful to include identical pages facing you so you can read them or comment on them without turning the presenter away from the client and losing eye contact with them.

Ask questions as you deliver your presentation and respond to any perceived reservations which the client may have.

Watch out for buying signals and make sure you recognise them. Some people find it difficult to stop talking and are so intent on delivering their prepared presentation they do not notice that the client is trying to book!

### RECOGNISING BUYING SIGNALS

The client's body language is one way of judging how interested they are. If they cross their arms and leave them that way, you can be fairly certain you are not getting through to them. More open, positive body language such as nods of understanding and approval mean you are saying what they want to hear.

Any enquiries about prices or requests for more details about your accommodation are effectively buying signals. All you need to do is deliver the right answer so they can buy. Even minor worries or reservations are buying signals

Sales activities

– DEVELOPING SALES
  SKILLS

– MAKING
  APPOINTMENTS

– PLANNING THE SALES
  MEETING

– AT THE SALES
  MEETING

– RECOGNISING BUYING
  SIGNALS

because they indicate that if you remove those, the way will be clear for you to do business together.

Towards the end of your presentation or when you have recognised good buying signals, you should start to make some minor assumptions. These might include asking if the client would like you to arrange credit facilities for them, or asking which of their clients would most enjoy your accommodation.

At this stage you may find that they once again raise some small objections. Stress the benefits and be open with the client. Ask them if they would be ready to book with you if you can sort out those minor problems.

Once you have finished your presentation, don't be afraid of asking for bookings or asking whether they are likely to be working with you in the near future. Don't chatter to break a silence. When faced with a short pause or silence, many people will use the occasion to buy!

Experiencing your product at first hand will help to convince the client and seal a future bond between you. Offer to arrange for them to sample it, either alone or with their family. You should either set a date there and then, or send complimentary vouchers to them as soon as possible.

Before you leave make sure you have agreed what the follow-up to the meeting will be. Don't just leave with a vague, 'I'll look forward to hearing from you.' This puts the ball in the client's court and is not very positive. If you can agree that you will take specific action by a certain date you will have another chance to impress with your efficiency and the sale will once again be in your hands.

## The best promotional tool of all – word of mouth

The most effective promotional tool is word of mouth and recommendations from existing guests – it's free and credible. 'Going the extra mile' instead of providing basic standards of service can provide a memorable visitor experience and make all the difference to your business. Visitors are much more likely to recommend you to others.

The hospitality industry is a people industry and it is ultimately you and your staff who will make a good or bad impression on your guests. Helpful, efficient and knowledgeable staff can make a big difference between a mediocre visitor experience and a memorable and rewarding one. Think about whether you can provide any or all of the following aspects in your customer service.

Provide a warm welcome and create a favourable first impression when guests arrive. Greet them as soon as possible and make the first few seconds count. Remember that it's not just what you say that communicates a message: tone of voice and body language are important too.

Be prepared to take the initiative and don't wait for guests to make the first move. Deal with complaints and other difficult situations quickly and aim to resolve problems to the guest's satisfaction. Try to make sure that all guest contact and transactions end on a positive note.

Memory of the total experience is what your guest will take away. Cleanliness, staff efficiency and the overall comfort of the bedroom and bathroom are of paramount importance. Guests also remember staff attitude, atmosphere and attention to detail. Things done exceptionally well differentiate one accommodation provider from another and give it a competitive edge.

Sales activities

- DEVELOPING SALES SKILLS
- MAKING APPOINTMENTS
- PLANNING THE SALES MEETING
- AT THE SALES MEETING
- RECOGNISING BUYING SIGNALS

The best promotional tool of all – word of mouth

# Chapter 6
# Internet marketing

The internet has already become an essential promotional tool for the tourism and leisure industry. Travel is one of the fastest growing and most commercially successful sectors of e-commerce. Holiday/travel is the number three reason for consumers going online and the most common online purchases are 'travel, accommodation and holidays'.* Many sites still fail to harness some of the true benefits of internet marketing.

This chapter looks at use of the internet as a promotional tool and how it can be integrated into your marketing strategy, as well as offering concrete advice on how to promote your site.

* *Sources*: Enjoy England 2005/Office of National Statistics.

## Taking advantage of the benefits of the internet

The first websites to be developed by accommodation providers were little more than online brochures. They used almost the same format, same information and same photographs as the original brochure. If your site is still like this, it is time to upgrade and take advantage of the differences between the internet and other promotional tools.

Accommodation is a perishable product. If you do not sell a bedroom on a particular night, you will never have the opportunity to recoup that lost revenue. The internet can help you to sell last minute as well as in advance. Your brochure will go out of date, but there is no reason why your website shouldn't always have the very latest information on it. You can react very quickly to changing conditions by adapting prices, information and offers instantly.

Perhaps the biggest advantage of the internet, and one which is often overlooked, is the fact that it is a one-to-one marketing method. Traditional print material is viewed sequentially – readers flick through brochures to find details which are relevant to them. Information on the internet is presented according to demand, so in theory at least, the user only sees the information that is directly relevant to them. Websites are viewed on a screen just a few inches from the users' eyes so it feels like a very personal means of communication.

It is hard to develop separate messages for each market segment within traditional tools such as advertisements or brochures. There is simply not enough space. This is not the case with the web, where there is even the option of developing sub-sites or separate areas for each segment. If you wanted to, you could create an area with a totally different look and feel, aimed solely at the children of guests.

Rather than simply presenting information in a listings or directory-style format, you can offer information sorted according to themes and motivations, or personal situations.

The interactive nature of the internet means there is potential to make a much greater impact than with traditional print media: we remember 10% of what we read, 30% of what we see, 50% of what we see and hear, but 90% of what we see, hear and do. The internet is a multi-media experience, with the capacity to present information through text, graphics, sound and video. It is interactive – every time a user wants information, they have to click to receive it.

You don't have to have your own website to benefit from internet promotion. If your accommodation has been quality inspected, you can obtain an entry on the www.enjoyengland.com and www.visitbritain.com websites or those of your local or regional tourist board. You are more likely to receive bookings from people looking for accommodation online if you at least have an email address but if not, you can simply give your telephone number.

Some sites such as those developed by the regional tourist boards and destination management organisations enable you to set an allocation of rooms which they can then sell on your behalf online, sending you reservations by fax or phone. However most of these systems increasingly expect you to have email to receive bookings.

There are numerous sites such as www.smoothhound.co.uk which act as a kind of directory of accommodation. You can add basic details of your accommodation to such sites for a relatively low cost, usually paying around the price of a one night stay in a twin room in your establishment, in return to a year's representation on that site. The advantage of this is that you can obtain a web-based presence at a fraction of the cost of developing a web site from scratch. In effect, this is simply another form of advertising, offering you coverage in return for a payment, possibly opening up new markets. It is just as important to monitor the effectiveness of entries in internet directories as with any other form of advertising.

There are two main disadvantages to relying on directories and other organisations to provide your web presence. The first is that most visitors using the internet prefer to click straight through to the accommodation provider's own website for more information and are dubious about those that don't have sites. The second is that if some-one is using a search engine (see later in this chapter) to find accommodation, your establishment is unlikely to be directly listed within the search engines so you might miss out on some potential bookings. When you rely on online directories, you are competing much more directly with other local providers.

If you have a small establishment and are happy with the level of bookings you get, you might be content to remain as you are and just use third parties to give you a web presence. If not, then now might be the time to think about using email and developing a website.

It's easier and cheaper than ever before to get online. You can buy a new computer with printer for as little as £300 and many companies offer deals which include all the necessary software already loaded and ready to use. If you'd like some help to learn to use a computer, you can get good advice and information from Business Link (www.businesslink.co.uk or telephone 0845 600 9006) and Learn Direct (www.learndirect.co.uk or telephone 0800 101 901). Many of the services they offer are completely free of charge to small businesses.

If you are thinking about developing a website for the first time, it is well-worth attending one of the half day courses offered by organisations like Business Link so you have an overview of what is needed.

## Developing a website

Websites need to be continually redeveloped and improved. Sometimes this can be done through a few minor tweaks and updates. If you are thinking about redeveloping your site, it might be easier to do this from scratch. This section will help you to do that.

### PLANNING THE SITE

You will save time and money if you draw up a detailed plan and contents for your website before contacting a designer. The first step is to list your target markets and then list all the different types of information each market is likely to be looking for, and the kind of functions your website will need to fulfil.

Think about the order in which they might need information and which content will be the most important, so you can avoid hiding essential details in the innermost pages of the website. Once someone has booked a hotel and is perhaps just about to set off to go there, it can be frustrating to have to search through pages and pages to find the address and location details. Remember that people will use your site at different stages of the buying process.

It often helps to draw a diagram showing the information your targets will look for, when and in what order, so you can create a site plan. This will usually look like a tree diagram or organisational chart. Indicate how everything will link together and the sequence of material.

Take a good look at your competitors' websites. Are there any lessons you can learn from them? Make a list of their best and worst features.

Make sure you have clarified who will have control of your site. In its initial stages you will probably need the support of a technically skilled resource, which might include the IT department of your company or an external consultant. Make sure though that the key responsibility for the website rests with someone who understands marketing. It is an additional channel of communication with your customers, not a technical tool.

### BUDGETING FOR YOUR WEBSITE

You can get a designer to build a website for anything upwards of around £1,500, but it could cost quite a bit more if you want to take bookings online. Some designers offer a budget service for around £400 which gives you several simple templates to choose from in order to create a simplified site, which may well be perfectly adequate for smaller accommodation providers. Whatever budget you allocate, bear in mind that there will not only be a one-off set-up cost, but also ongoing operational and development costs. These will include the cost of maintaining your domain name and the space where your site is hosted, as well as improvements to the site.

If you do decide that you need to keep costs to a minimum, you can build your own site using easy-to-use software such as Macromedia's *Dreamweaver*. These packages do not require you to learn html (the code behind most websites) or have any real programming skills.

However, unless you are particularly skilled in that area, it would be worthwhile getting a designer to devise a suitable layout for your home page so you present a professional image. You can then follow the suggested layout for subsequent pages and focus your attention on ensuring that you have appropriate content for the site.

You can also keep costs down (and maintain control) by making sure that you can update the site yourself. Beware of designers who say that you need to learn special software. Software like *Dreamweaver* is very easy to learn and use.

When you are ready to choose a website developer, ask industry colleagues and your local tourist board for their recommendations. You may be able to get additional support from Business LInk.

### DESIGN GUIDELINES

- Don't be too clever. Assume a lower rather than higher level of technical knowledge on the part of your users. Don't use animations and other innovations just for the sake of it. It is, however, worth considering virtual or 360 degree tours because visitors really do like to know how a place feels, and this is an ideal way of showing them.
- It is useful to stick with conventional design, which means mirroring the majority of sites that use a left-hand menu for navigation purposes. Only underline words when they are actually links, or make the links within your site very clear.
- Make sure the pages of your website are easy to print out, as many users still prefer to print pages of text and read them offline later or hand them to others.
- Images and photographs can bring your website to life. You can provide supplementary images within a gallery section. Web users want as much information as possible, and thanks to digital cameras, it is now very easy to add extra images.
- Research suggests that only about 10% of users scroll beyond the information immediately seen on their screen. This has several implications. If your site requires the user to read a lot of text, make sure you layer the information, putting the most important first.

- Your home page needs to make a strong impact. Use a friendly, bright and very clear style and make the purpose of the site immediately obvious. If it is possible to make online bookings on your site, say so and provide a direct link to that area. If not, either provide a link to another site where bookings can be made or to your contact details.

## Writing copy for websites

You will need to write shorter, more concise copy for the website because users tend to scan information rather than scroll through long pages of text. It is a good idea to break up and layer the information for your website, according to different consumer needs, taking advantage of the interactivity of the internet to present content in the order that the user wants. A series of short passages of information, just a few clicks away from each other, is the most appropriate way to present content on the internet.

Websites that encourage users to feel most positive about the companies behind them usually have three levels of content:

1   Core information about the company's product or services. For example, a hotel would include details about rooms and other facilities, prices and perhaps an online booking facility.
2   Enhanced information that sets the product or service in context or helps the user to feel more informed, even if this content is slightly peripheral to the actual product or service being promoted. A hotel might include a currency converter, weather forecast or links to more information about the location of the hotel.
3   Inspirational or persuasive information which encourages the user to imagine why they might want to buy that product and find reasons for doing so. A hotel's website might have plenty of information about things to do in the area, local history and recommendations for local pubs or attractions.

If you deal with people from all over the world, do you need to offer translated versions of your website? You can either get your site professionally translated or link to one of the translation sites that automate the process. Their version will never be as good as one translated by a mother-tongue professional, but will at least show you are trying to be helpful. Another option is to offer a one-page summary of your facilities in each of the languages of your target markets.

### CREATING A MEDIA-FRIENDLY WEBSITE

Journalists use the web to research their stories. You can make their job easier, and increase the chances of them featuring your accommodation, by providing a special media or press centre within your website. This could include current and previous press releases, a brief profile of your company, your staff and any other interesting facts, and downloadable high resolution images.

### CHECKLIST FOR YOUR SITE

Following this checklist will help you to make sure your site is easy to use and has a clear, attractive design.

- Is the navigation clear?
- Is the menu in an obvious place, easy to see and on each page, so it is possible to get to all areas of the site in the minimum number of 'clicks'?
- Does the site follow the same design throughout?
- Is relevant information presented and requested at appropriate times? For example, users will not want to give their credit card details before they have had the chance to search for services they are interested in.
- Is most information just three clicks away from the home page?
- Is the site really interactive?
- Does it make it possible for the user to obtain only the information they are interested in?
- Is the language clear?
- Does it avoid jargon that only some users will understand?
- Does it give clear, concise instructions to users?
- Is the text easy to read and understand?

- Is the content presented in 'bite-sized' chunks?
- If the site asks for data from the user, is it easy to input?
- Is it obvious exactly what is being asked?
- Does the site help to build your brand and overall identity?
- Is it instantly recognisable and in keeping with your other promotional activities?
- Is the design relevant to your target markets?
- Are principal concerns such as those about privacy addressed within the site?
- Is there an opportunity for users to give feedback?
- Would they be confident that they will receive a speedy response?
- Is the site updated at regular intervals?

## Promoting your website

The first easy step is to make sure your domain name is memorable and easy to spell. If you think there is a better domain name than the one you currently have, it is pretty cheap to register another one and 'point' it to your site. You will not need to change your site and the old address will still work, but you could gradually introduce the new address. You can also register different domain names to use in different kinds of promotion, all pointing to the same website.

Short names are easier to remember, and there is less danger that users will make a mistake when typing the name and risk not finding you. If your name is one that is often spelt incorrectly, it can be worthwhile registering the incorrect version as well as the correct one.

Domain names are case insensitive but are usually given as lower case. Sometimes it is a good idea to write the domain name with some capitals in it to make it easier to read and remember, for example, **www.VisitBritain.com**.

If you ask someone else such as a website designer to register the domain name on your behalf, make sure that the certificate of registration is in your name and not theirs so that you actually own the site.

Do make sure your reception and frontline staff have seen your site, and encourage them to look at it from time to time so they can refer potential guests to specific parts of it. Encourage your staff to pass on any feedback they receive about the site, and to suggest new features for it. Frontline staff will be able to help you compile lists of 'Frequently Asked Questions' for the site. Staff photos will help to personalise your site.

When you advertise your accommodation you no longer need to put all relevant details into one small advertisement. You can use something like a strong photograph to grab attention and then just a website address for more information. If you use a different website entry point (for example, **www.hotelname.com/families** or **www.hotelname.com/couples**) for each advertisement, you will be able to see which advertisements are the most effective. Remember to include an enticing strapline saying what your site does and how users will benefit, instead of just giving your name and website address.

You can use public relations' activities to attract people to your site and promote your accommodation at the same time. For example, you might want to launch a competition that is accessed via your website, or perhaps you could conduct an online survey and then issue a press release with the results. The media seem to love quirky survey findings and the sample size need not be particularly large.

## Promoting through search engines

One of the main ways in which users will find your site is via a search engine. The name 'search engine' is often used interchangeably to describe actual search engines and 'directories' even though they are not the same. The main difference lies in the way that listings are compiled.

Promoting through
search engines

– HOW SEARCH
  ENGINES WORK

– TIPS TO IMPROVE
  YOUR RANKINGS

– ADVERTISING WITH
  SEARCH ENGINES

### HOW SEARCH ENGINES WORK

Some of the more famous so-called search engines such as **www.yahoo.com** are actually directories. These are compiled by humans, who either write short reviews of sites, or base listings on short descriptions of sites submitted by site owners. True search engines such as Google create their listings automatically. They 'crawl' the web, scanning sites and pages to compile listings.

Each search engine has its own special software that sifts through the index and determines the rank of websites in its listings. This is why your website will be ranked differently by different search engines. Some search engines also index pages more frequently than others. Some search engines combine several techniques, using humans and automatic crawlers.

You can find more information about how each search engine or directory works by going to their 'help' pages. If you look at the foot of most search engines they have an 'add a site' link, leading to a simple form for submission. Sites such as **www.searchenginewatch.com** also contain useful information to help you understand how search engines work. It can be time-consuming to optimise your site, but spending a day on this every few months could help you to increase your search engine rankings, and therefore your sales.

Although search engines work in different ways, most of them determine the relevance of websites using similar criteria. These are some of the elements they look for:

- Pages with keywords appearing in their title are more relevant than others.
- Pages where the keywords appear near the top of the page, in the headline or first paragraphs are more relevant.
- The content of the page is important – pages that mention the keywords more frequently and within their true context, are likely to achieve a higher ranking.
- Other criteria include link popularity. Link popularity is used to some extent by all the search engines to determine how sites should be ranked. The link popularity of your site is determined by the number of websites that link to your site. You can find out who is linking to your site by using **www.linkpopularity.com**.

- Meta tags are important for some search engines. When they were first developed, some website owners repeated keywords many times in order to increase their rank in the listings. Search engines now recognise when these deliberate attempts are made to foil them
- Google is now the most popular search engine in the UK, mainly because its search results are so accurate. Its ranking system also considers how useful other searchers have found the findings.

### TIPS TO IMPROVE YOUR RANKINGS

You will need to identify relevant keywords for search engine registration, and to use them on your site. These should be at least two words long – focusing on just one word will mean that you are in enormous competition with many other sites, but choosing two will increase the relevance of your site in many searches.

For example, the word 'hotel' will return thousands of sites, whereas the words 'London hotels' will narrow down the search. However, there will still be many listings for these two keywords, so words such as 'Central' and/or 'town-house', and/or 'budget' might be added.

Search engines cannot read tables in the same way as they are seen on the page. They break the tables in such a way that keywords may be pushed lower down the page. The only solution to this problem is to use meta tags, although not all search engines use them.

If you use image map links instead of text links you will find that some search engines will not follow the links to pages beyond the home page, which are often the most relevant. One way of counteracting this is to include a site map page with text links to all areas of your website. Ensure that you include plenty of good internal links on your site.

The complexities of search engine submission have led to the growth of an army of consultants who claim to be able to improve your chances of a high ranking in the listings. Most of them use very similar techniques to the ones mentioned here, which take as much time as skill, and really depend on your intimate knowledge of your customers and how their minds work to know instinctively which keywords they will search on. Do bear in mind that it can take up to three months before your submitted pages appear in some search engine listings.

If you are tempted to use a 'web optimisation consultancy', why not search for one with various search engines? Presumably if they are really good at their job, their site will be placed at the top of the list.

Once your site is listed, don't assume it will always appear within the listings in the same place. You will need to keep checking it and resubmitting from time to time.

If you want to promote your site internationally, you should consider submitting your site to each country version, as they do not automatically take the sites from their American or UK partners. It can also help to have a domain name which is relevant to other countries.

### ADVERTISING WITH SEARCH ENGINES

You can further enhance your search engine rankings by advertising with the search engines. This is known in the industry as 'paid search marketing' and should not be confused with how high up the list your site appears in the 'natural' search results. Your site's listing in the natural results is free but there is no guarantee that you will appear at the top of the page, or even on the first page. The majority of people will limit their searching to the first page of results on the search engine of their choice.

Paid search marketing plugs this gap, enabling you to pay the search engine to place a small advert and link on the first page of the results.

The way this works is straightforward, although the different search engines have slightly different implementations. Let us take Google as an example. Imagine you run an upmarket hotel in the Yorkshire Dales which is known for its good food. Google allows you to 'bid' on the keywords that you think people might use to find a site like yours. This can cost anything from a few pence to several pounds but you are able to set the amount you wish to pay. You could bid on 'Yorkshire Dales good food' and tell Google that you are willing to pay up to 50p per click.

When someone uses Google and enters the very same keywords that you bid on, then your advert will appear. This will usually be on the right-hand side of the page under the 'sponsored links'. The position of your advert (first place or fifth place) will depend on whether someone else has outbid you on those keywords as well as the relevance and popularity of your site. You do not necessarily need to be in first place to get people clicking through to your site. Each time someone used those keywords and saw your paid search ranking and then clicked through to your site, Google would charge you 50p.

By bidding on numerous keyword combinations (including misspellings) which you think people might use to look for a site like yours, you can build up steady traffic to your site.

You do need to track the effectiveness of your paid searches and compare it with other methods. For example, imagine you currently spend £10 for every booking you receive through a booking agent. You could therefore also aim to pay up to £10 per internet booking received via paid searches. If you were paying Google 50p per click it would mean that as long as you get at least one booking for every 20 people who click on your site, then you are paying the same or less as with the booking agent.

You might notice that a certain set of keywords are not reaping any returns, so you could either drop them completely or lower the maximum bid you are willing to pay. Although there is a constant element of trial and error, you can change your search engine account settings online and the results are instantaneous. You must, however, keep checking the effectiveness so you do not find later that you are being billed for non-productive clicks through to your website. If you are not managing to convert many click-throughs to bookings, you might also need to ask yourself if the website needs improving or the booking process needs to be made easier.

It is not difficult to set up keyword advertising. Just go to the search engine you are interested in, and you will find that you can select keywords and pay immediately with your credit card. This can all be done online, and there are numerous tutorials and support mechanisms so you can do it all yourself without having to pay for additional help.

## Reciprocal links

Part of the power of the internet is the way that so many sites are linked together so users can follow one thread to find almost endless information on the subjects they are interested in. Arranging reciprocal links between your site and others is another cost-free way of promoting your site and adding value.

Use the main search engines to look for sites connected to your business, such as attractions in your area, pubs and other places of interest. Use the results and look at the top 10 or 20 sites.

You will need to decide whether you are going to place the links at relevant points within your text and pages, or group them altogether in one part of the site, like a directory.

It usually seems most natural and appropriate to put the links in context by placing them within the main body of your site, such as within a page about things to do. Your guests will also appreciate this additional information, which they will perceive as better customer service.

Try to think of all the extra information you think your site users would benefit from having and research the sites. Don't provide links to sites you have not checked out because your users will see links as a kind of recommendation from you. If your links are irrelevant or inappropriate they might start to doubt the other services you offer. Make sure you keep checking the links from time to time to make sure they still exist, and invite feedback from users about your existing links and their suggestions for new ones.

Contact all the sites you would like to link to, giving a brief description of what your site does and the kind of users you target, and ask if they will consider reciprocal links. Make sure you let the webmaster of the sites you are linking to know that you have already created a link to them, and remind them to link to your site, suggesting the most appropriate page on your site for their link.

## Online booking

There is an increasing expectation from consumers that they should be able to buy or make bookings on tourism and leisure websites.

Developing a website which is capable of accepting online bookings or acting as a shop-front is potentially complex because of the need to build a suitable 'back-office' system, develop a secure site and accept online payments. You are recommended to seek more detailed technical advice before embarking on the development of an e-commerce site.

If you are keen to accept online bookings, you basically have three options:

1 Work with an established online booking agent who has already developed suitable systems and can incorporate your hotel into their system. This means that you potentially benefit from much greater and broader exposure. The downside is that you will be promoted along with your competitors and it is harder to maintain your own identity. You might decide to use this option and one of the other two listed below as well. More information about how to connect to national, regional and local tourism websites is given later in this section.
2 Buy an off-the-shelf software solution – this is usually cheaper and easier than developing your own solution from scratch. Most systems are very comprehensive but more suited to selling products than services. Some of them use templates so can be difficult to tailor to your precise needs. They can look out of place within some sites and since many of the solutions were first developed in the US, they may have an American slant.

Promoting through search engines

– HOW SEARCH ENGINES WORK

– TIPS TO IMPROVE YOUR RANKINGS

– ADVERTISING WITH SEARCH ENGINES

Reciprocal links

Online booking

3 Develop your own site with the help of a programmer – this will be the most expensive option but in the long run will probably be the most productive because you will have a tailor-made system which is completely suited to your needs.

## Distribution via international, national, regional and local tourism websites

VisitBritain and its regional and commercial partners recognise that the key to success for most businesses is being able to offer consumers the opportunity to look for tourism products online and book them. It also wants to make it easier for visitors to find products and make decisions about their holiday, and is doing this through its websites: **www.visitbritain.com** and **www.enjoyengland.com**. Eventually consumers will be able to assemble their own tour through these websites and book much of it online.

VisitBritain has a huge National Tourism Product Database which processes information from many different sources such as regional tourist board systems, and then feeds VisitBritain's family of websites so participating accommodation providers will effectively have domestic and global reach.

Individual accommodation providers can benefit from these partnerships. You first of all need to make sure your accommodation has been quality assessed (see Chapter 9) and then it will automatically be included on the National Tourism Product Database.

Once your accommodation is in the Database you will be able to check, amend and add more details and images via your regional or local tourism partner. Contact details for these are given at the end of this chapter.

If you offer your accommodation for online booking through a booking agent who is part of VisitBritain's network of national, regional and local tourism partners and commercial consolidators, you can offer potential visitors the opportunity to check the availability and price of your accommodation through VisitBritain's websites: www.visitbritain.com and www.enjoyengland.com. These visitors will then be seamlessly transferred to the website of your booking agent to complete their booking.

It is important to stress that these tourism and commercial websites will not replace your website. They will simply help more people to find your product and to book it.

The National Tourism Product Database also feeds information on attractions and events through to VisitBritain's websites. Further information on who to contact to ensure your attraction or event is included in the National Tourism Product Database is given at the end of this chapter.

## Concerns about privacy

Many people are concerned about their privacy and the potential of being bombarded by unwanted E-mails. It is unlikely that this concern will go away, so if you want potential guests to give you their E-mail address or submit any other information through your website, it makes sense to include a brief privacy statement on your site.

A privacy statement can be as simple or complex as you think necessary for your target markets. If you are just asking users of your site to register to receive further information, you will probably need to give them a small incentive to do so (this might be the quality of the information itself) and to explain why you are collecting the data, and what it will and will not be used for. It is a good idea to include an explanation of the benefits to your customers when collecting such information. These benefits might include better services and offers (try to be specific), improved navigation of the site, more personalised services and so on.

Here is an example of a privacy statement. You will need to rewrite it to take into consideration particular aspects of your own business and website. You are recommended to take legal advice in order to draft the most appropriate information.

Online booking

Distribution via international, national, regional and local tourism websites

Concerns about privacy

'When anyone uses this website our web server automatically creates log files containing technical information about their connection. This includes such things as how long people use the site for and what pages they visit, but no personally identifiable information is created. We use this technical information to understand how people use this site, and to improve the site's content.

If you E-mail us with a request for more information, we will record your E-mail address for future mailings. However, we DO NOT make this information available to any other organisation. If you wish us to remove your E-mail address from our records, please let us know and we will willingly do so straight away.'

It is also a common-sense policy to display a list of terms and conditions on your site so customers can see the terms under which they are making a booking before they commit themselves.

## Monitoring the effectiveness of your website

The internet is one of the most measurable promotional methods. You can track a customer once they visit your site, assess how long they are spending in each area of the site and trace these patterns whenever they visit the site again. If we were to compare this to traditional direct mail, we would be able to tell whether a potential customer had opened the envelope you posted to them, which paragraphs they read and which inserts they put in the bin, as well as knowing whether they open any future mailings you send them. You can also find out how users heard about your site, without having to ask them but by simply interpreting site log files.

Your Internet Service Provider should provide you with log files or statistics free of charge. You will probably need to go to their website to access them. Here are some of the common pieces of information you are likely to see and how to interpret them.

Many people speak about **hits** or **requests**, but these are not such a good measurement. Every time a page is requested, a hit is recorded and every graphic on that page records another hit. So a page without pictures would record one hit, but a page with 15 photographs would show as 16 hits. When someone boasts about a high number of website hits it could simply mean they have a lot of images on their pages.

It is helpful to know about **referrers**. Your server logs the sites that lead a user to your site. The referrer report shows you who has links to you and how much traffic they send.

**Search strings** are particularly useful. They show the actual words that people are using with search engines such as Google or Yahoo. You will then know which keywords might be particularly useful for online advertising and site descriptions.

**IP (Internet Protocol) addresses** are useful because they can give you an indication of how many unique users or visitors come to your website. Every computer has a unique Internet Protocol (IP) address when it is online. Some computers have a permanent IP address and others are assigned a temporary IP address each time they log on. The site statistics in your log shows how many unique IP addresses made requests to the server. This number may be lower than the actual number of individuals using your site because some homes and offices share an IP address, so it does not show each individual person.

**Entry** and **exit pages** are shown. This means that whenever a visit is triggered or ended, the server logs the page the visitor entered or exited. If you have done some advertising and given a website address within the site itself rather than the home page, this information could help you monitor the effectiveness of the ad.

Concerns about privacy

Monitoring the effectiveness of your website

## Spring clean your website

Chances are you've already got a website but it could be much more effective. Here are some guidelines to help you spruce up and improve your site.

Remember the reasons for having a site in the first place. Try to re-cap what they were and use them to double check the website's effectiveness. Was it because you wanted to take online bookings? If so, does every page make it clear that guests can book online?

Get your receptionist or someone who has a lot of guest contact to jot down a list of the most frequently asked questions. You might want to divide these into queries about the accommodation itself and those about the local area. Once you've got this list take a look through your website. Are the answers to these frequently asked questions clear and obvious? Do you need to re-write some sections of your website or create a 'frequently asked questions' section?

Using your list of target markets (Chapter 4) go through your website and consider whether you've included appropriate information for each of those markets. Do you describe your accommodation in a way that would appeal to your chosen segments?

List the information that your markets are likely to be looking for and in what order. Then systematically go through your website and consider whether the information is available where guests would expect to find it. How many clicks away is the most popular information? Your website hosting company should be able to provide you with statistics to show you which pages are the most popular. Are these the ones you'd expect to be most frequently visited? Sometimes the pages you'd expect to be popular aren't – this could be because the navigation isn't as straightforward as it should be.

continued

You might need to re-order the information to make sure that the most important content is easy to see. What information should be seen first and what could be presented at a later stage?

Consider using your own 'home made' focus groups. You'll need to choose people who correspond to each of your target markets. It's a good idea to choose couples or friends as they often make comments to each other that can be helpful to you. Ask them to browse around the site and comment on what they see and then to perform a couple of set tasks. Make notes on their comments. How many clicks does it take them to obtain specific information and how easy is it to find? How could the site be improved?

Bear in mind there are probably two distinct types of visitor: 1) those who are ready to book and want do so as fast as possible and 2) those who still need to be convinced and want some additional information before they do so. Do you offer them both appropriate information and menu links?

Does your website provide a strong call to action on each and every page? For example, 'book here' with a link to either the booking part of the site or your telephone number and E-mail in big bold writing.

Take a close look at all the photographs within the website. Do they reflect the right image? Could some of them be improved simply by cropping out extraneous detail? Images are very important and often the first thing that users look at so make sure that you have powerful photography.

## Glossary of terms

This brief glossary of terms should ensure that you are not completely bamboozled by the 'techies'.

**ad server**   Software which delivers advertisements to relevant website pages, and keeps track of advertising inventory and performance.

**ad views/impressions**   Number of times a page with an online advertisement on it has been viewed.

**backend system**   Any part of a website that the user has no direct contact with, such as automated credit card processing or distribution system.

**bandwidth**   The capacity for traffic on any computer network (including the internet) or the maximum amount of information passed over a connection in one second, usually measured in bps (bits per second).

**bookmark**   Virtual bookmarks work in the same way as real ones. They record a website or URL so you can go straight to it at a later date.

**browser**   Viewer for the World Wide Web, or in other words, window through which the internet is viewed. The most popular ones are Microsoft's Internet Explorer and Netscape's Navigator.

**caching**   This is the process of storing frequently requested information either on a server or special sites within a network to avoid 'traffic jams' on the web at peak access times.

**chatroom**   An online facility for real-time communication between people over the internet, usually achieved through typed conversations.

**click**   Click (or double click) of the computer mouse to access information via a link.

**click-through rates (*or* CTR)**   The click-through rate measures the number of times an advertisement is clicked on, so is effectively a way of measuring interest in an advertisement.

**cookie**    A cookie is a piece of software which records information about users. It holds this information until such time that the server requests it. For example, if you are browsing around a virtual shop, each time you place an item in your basket the information is stored by the cookie until you decide to buy and the server requests the purchase information.

**CPM**    The cost per thousand advertisement impressions is the usual measure for online advertising.

**DNS (or Domain Name Server)**    A server that performs address verification on the internet, finding the right computer to connect to for access to websites and E-mail.

**domain name**    The website address or Universal Resource Locator, part of the naming hierarchy of the internet.

**extranet**    A web-style network that is used by a specific but often broad range of people, such as a group of suppliers and customers or particular industry. It often branches off a company's internal network.

**FAQ (or Frequently Asked Questions)**    Lists of Frequently Asked Questions (and their answers) allow the user to search for a query that somebody has already found the answer to. Many websites now have an FAQ section, cutting down on some of the need for customer service call centres.

**filetype**    Commonly a three- or four-letter extension to the end of a file name designating the file type. There are hundreds in existence, and new ones are constantly being invented. Examples are: .txt (text file); .gif (Graphics Interchange Format).

**firewall**    A means of protecting websites and systems from trespassers and 'hackers'. A firewall is a secure software barrier against unauthorised intrusion or data theft.

**Flash**    A technology developed by Macromedia to create small (in terms of file size) animations.

**FTP (or File Transfer Protocol)**    A method used to transfer computer files from one computer to another over the internet. It usually refers to the process of transferring HTML files and graphics files (such as GIF and JPEG) from your computer to the computer which hosts your website.

**home page**    The first page a surfer sees when they run their browser or when they access your site.

**host**    You usually connect to a host computer whenever you use the internet.

**HTML (*or* HyperText Markup Language)**    The language of the web, HTML, is the code inserted in a file intended for display on a web browser to indicate how and what should be displayed.

**HTTP (*or* HyperText Transport Protocol)**    Used on the World Wide Web since 1990, this application-level protocol is essential for the distribution of information throughout the Web.

**hyperlink**    Hyperlinks are highlighted text or images which, when selected (usually by clicking the mouse button), follow a link to another page. Hyperlinks can also be used to automatically download other files as well as sounds and video clips.

**image map**    An image with clickable 'hot spots', allowing several hyperlinks from a single image file. For example, the image could be of a country split into different areas, each of which could be clickable and hyperlink to a larger view of that specific area, or link to further information about each area.

**Internet Service Provider (*or* ISP)**    A company that supplies access to the internet.

**intranet**    A web-style network that sits within the boundaries of a single company. However, many intranets span more than one location (for companies with more than one office) and/or can be accessed from anywhere.

**IP address**    This number refers to the physical location of individual web or mail servers. Domain names provide an alias for these which are much easier to understand, for example, **www.websitename.com** rather than 104.66.27.33. While many domain names can apply to one computer, a computer can have only one IP address.

**JPEG *or* jpeg (Joint Photographic Experts Group)**
A standard of image compression developed especially for use on the internet. Most photographic images can be

highly compressed using this method, without greatly diminishing image quality.

**links**   Links are the connections between hypertext pages. Every time you click on highlighted text to go to another page you are following a link.

**menu**   Used for navigating web pages, the menu is usually a list of options and links appearing on the home page of a website.

**meta tags**   HTML tags which surround certain words so that search engines can identify keywords when performing a search.

**microsite**   A small or sub-site usually contained within a larger website, often designed for a specific purpose, such as responding to particular enquiries.

**modem**   A device used to connect most home users to the internet, a modem is the interface between the user's computer and telephone line. It is short for modulator demodulator.

**network**   Any number of computers which have been interconnected to allow information to be transferred among them, ranging from a small office to the internet itself.

**opt-in mailing**   A mailing which is sent to pre-qualified groups of people, who have agreed to be on a mailing list.

**pixel**   Short for picture element, a pixel is a single point or 'dot' in a graphics image. The number of pixels decides the picture density or quality. The more pixels, the clearer the image.

**plug-ins**   Plug-ins are programmes which can be installed and used as part of your web browser. Although they are generally easy to download, many surfers resist using them. Shockwave and RealAudio are examples of plug-ins required for audio and video.

**portal**   A term for websites which have all the services people are likely to use online, for example, search engines, chatrooms, online shopping. They are all gathered together on one site and link to other sites.

**protocol**   Standards governing the transfer of information between computers.

**rich media**   Rich media means that it includes multimedia such as sound and possibly video. Rich media is increasingly popular with advertisers.

**server**   Computer or software on a computer which allows other computers to access it via a network or over the internet.

**signature**   The automatic addition of a few lines at the foot of an E-mail. These usually consist of the sender's E-mail address, full name and other details.

**spam**   Unwanted or 'junk' E-mail.

**streaming**   Video or audio files sent in compressed form over the internet and displayed on the viewer's screen as they arrive.

**tag**   In HTML terms, a tag is used for marking-up text or coding it in various ways so that it is formatted in a web document. They are sometimes called 'markup tags'.

**upload**   Transfer of files from a local computer to a specified remote computer (as opposed to download where files are pulled off a remote machine). Once a website has been developed, it has to be uploaded to a host so the site can be seen by all internet users.

**URL (*or* Universal Resource Locator)**   The website address or domain name.

**virus**   A virus is similar to a 'bug' caught by humans. A virus can attack computers and hide anywhere where a computer stores information. They have the ability to transfer from computer to computer via E-mail or the internet and various other networks. A virus can do a number of things to a recipient, such as reformatting hard drives or destroying data.

**webmaster**   The person responsible for maintaining a website.

## VisitBritain online contact details

If you want to distribute your product through VisitBritain's websites, your first point of contact should be your national, regional or local tourism partner, details of who to contact can be found here: www.visitbritain.com/connect. To update or amend your accommodation, attraction or event details on VisitBritain, contact your national, regional or local data steward, details of which can be found here: www.visitbritain.com/datastewards

Glossary of terms

VisitBritain online
contact details

# Chapter 7

# Working with others to develop your business

Running your own business can be lonely and sometimes it is difficult to know where to turn or get advice. You might be surprised at just how much help is available. In this chapter we look at how you can work with tourist boards and tourist information centres to develop your business.

We have included some ideas about consortia marketing so you can join forces with other businesses in your area. In the final part of this chapter there is information about support agencies, training and working with consultants.

### Regional tourist boards

Chapter 1 explains the new structure for the regional tourist boards and Destination Management Organisations. In your region you might have the opportunity to belong to a regional tourist board, a sub-regional organisation and/or a local accommodation network or association. If you are not already a member of at least one of these, refer to the listings in the 'Additional information' section at the back of this book so you can find out more.

Membership fees vary from region to region, usually on a rising scale according to the size of the organisation. As well as giving you access to promotional activities organised by the national tourist boards and VisitBritain, membership services generally include:

- entries in publications, ranging from general destination guides to special interest brochures

- the opportunity to take stand space at selected exhibitions or to take part in workshops and seminars
- the opportunity to rent mailing lists
- sales leads
- opportunities to meet other members and share common concerns
- access to information and statistics about tourism activity in your area
- access to training courses
- joint purchasing schemes
- some marketing advice and expertise.

Regional tourist boards

- GETTING THE MOST FROM YOUR TOURIST BOARD

GETTING THE MOST FROM YOUR TOURIST BOARD

Before you commit yourself to joining your tourist board, ask exactly what benefits you will get from membership and be ready to take advantage of as many as possible.

You will probably be asked to fill in a form describing your services, in a set number of words. Make sure you do so, carefully considering the words you use. This short description is likely to be used in several publications going to a wide audience, so make sure you stress your Unique Selling Point and key benefits.

The key to benefiting from tourist board membership is involvement: go (or send a representative) to all your tourist board's meetings to which you are invited. You need to make sure you know what is happening in your area, use the opportunity to gather information about local developments and find out about your competitor's activities.

Introduce yourself to the staff, particularly those working in any tourist information centres, and invite them to sample your product so they understand what you are offering and can promote it.

## Tourist information centres

Tourist information centres

The network of tourist information centres are managed and run in a variety of ways, depending on the area of the country and funding structure. They are an important feature of the tourism industry, providing information and help for local residents, as well as domestic and overseas visitors.

The range of services provided varies, but usually includes information about places to visit and places to stay usually within about a 50-mile radius. Some tourist information centres offer an accommodation-booking service for the local area.

You can use tourist information centres as a channel of distribution and communication. It is certainly worth taking the time to build positive relationships with tourist information staff because they are in a position to influence the public, and pass on information about what visitors want.

Make sure you keep information centres supplied with the material they need to promote your accommodation. Don't hesitate to ask their advice when developing new aspects of your service, because they are in daily contact with the public and will have a good idea of what they want.

## Consortia marketing

When budgets are limited, it is often a good idea to combine forces with other like-minded people to promote together. You could either join an existing consortium of local accommodation providers and attractions, or if you can see a niche that is not currently being filled you might want to establish your own.

'Distinctly Different' is a group of unusual properties, such as converted mills, offering accommodation. They are all in different areas of the UK and undertake joint marketing activities on the principle that if someone stays in one property, they could then be convinced to stay in a similar one in another area. They are more capable of stimulating press coverage and raising their profile as a group than would be possible for individual properties.

Some consortia are established in order to share experiences and find solutions to common problems. They may be based on a very small local area, or could be properties with a common connection, such as being historic buildings.

If such a consortium or organisation does not already exist, there is nothing to stop you from setting up your own. Be sure of your objectives and what sort of membership you need. As soon as you start to recruit members, try to come up with a concrete plan of action and decide exactly what you are going to do so you do not just become a 'talking shop'. If possible, share tasks and responsibilities with others. This will reduce the workload on you and make more people feel fully involved.

Tourist information centres

Consortia marketing

## Additional support and help

Additional support and help

– THE IMPORTANCE OF TRAINING

– BUSINESS SUPPORT

There are numerous organisations that can offer you additional support and help. Some organisations focus on specific areas or regions. Your regional development agency should have details of these.

### THE IMPORTANCE OF TRAINING

Training and skills development are essential if the industry is to continue to grow. There are plenty of courses available on all aspects of tourism, hospitality and running a business. You can choose from practical one-day workshops and short courses, as well as year-long day release courses leading to a recognised qualification. The website **www.tourismtraining.info** includes a database of training providers.

### BUSINESS SUPPORT

In addition to training courses, there is now no shortage of support to help you run your business. Many of the government-funded organisations named in Chapter 12 can provide free and independent help and information.

Business Link is a government-funded organisation which specifically gives support to new and growing businesses employing fewer than 250 people. You can make an appointment to see one of their business advisors or download a wide range of fact sheets and helpful documents from their website **www.businesslink.gov.uk**. You will probably also find that your regional development agency has details of some local business support organisations.

## Setting up a marketing consortium

If one doesn't already exist in your area, why not establish your own marketing partnership? Some consortia are based on geographical criteria perhaps combining accommodation and visitor attractions from the same area. Others focus on something they have in common such as the Distinctly Different consortium, made up of unusual properties such as converted mills and lighthouses.

The benefits of being a member of a marketing consortium are many:

- Raising your profile – pooling resources means you can increase the impact of your promotional activities without spending more;
- Creating a collective identity – it can be hard for an individual accommodation provider to make a name for themselves or to create a strong identity;
- Discussion forum – sometimes all you need is an opportunity to use others as a sounding board or air common problems;
- Reduced costs – sharing stands at exhibitions and combining forces for familiarisation trips are just two ways you can share costs and undertake activities that might otherwise be beyond your budget;
- Shared expertise – consortia provide an opportunity for members to learn from each other or to combine resources and buy in specialist services.

If you decide to set up a consortium, there are a few pitfalls to avoid:

- Inertia – the stumbling block of many partnerships which simply become a 'talking shop' with no clear activities;
- Insufficient funds for activities – working in partnership can mean saving money but that doesn't mean that it doesn't cost anything;

continued

- Lack of direction – every partnership needs a driving force and specific benefits or services.

You can avoid the pitfalls by making sure you take these steps at the outset:

- Consider your objectives and try to set them down in writing, to serve as a kind of constitution for your group. As membership grows it's easy to get side-tracked. What size do you want the consortium to be? Will you have specific membership criteria?
- Decide how the consortium will be funded. It's sometimes possible to obtain grant aid at the beginning. Most consortia charge a membership fee which covers a set range of activities.
- Devise a plan of action that can be presented to members for approval and used as a yardstick to measure progress.
- Allocate tasks and responsibilities. You might want to consider employing someone as a co-ordinator to maintain momentum, even if only on a part-time basis.

Additional support and help

– THE IMPORTANCE OF TRAINING

– BUSINESS SUPPORT

Customer service is one of the most important aspects of any tourism business. The Welcome to Excellence series of training programmes, offered through regional tourist boards, is the most successful customer service training initiative in the UK.

There are now several one-day training programmes, which provide frontline staff and managers with the skills they need to provide high standards of service. These include 'Welcome Host', which is designed to improve standards of customer service given to visitors, and 'Welcome Host Plus', which builds on this. Welcome International gives people working in the industry greater confidence when meeting and greeting international visitors in another language. 'Welcome All' provides practical advice and guidance on service to customers with disabilities and special needs. 'Welcome Management' offers information for managers and supervisors who are responsible for leading a team of frontline staff. 'Welcome Line' concentrates on improving customer service by telephone. For more details see **www.welcometoexcellence.co.uk**.

## Working with consultants

There are some projects or aspects of promotional activities which you may find difficult or not have time to do yourself. There is an army of consultants waiting to help you – for a fee. Employing consultants should not necessarily be seen as the expensive option because it is cheaper than retaining full-time staff with specialist knowledge and skills.

It is worth shopping around to find someone who understands your business and is enthusiastic about it. Following these simple guidelines should help you to get value for money.

Make sure you have clearly defined objectives. Many unsuccessful consultancy relationships or projects are due to an inadequate briefing.

Ask for examples of past projects and if you can speak to past clients about the consultant's work. Find out if there is any kind of 'after-sales service'. What happens once the project is finished? Will you be able to ask advice about specific aspects at a later date without charge? Good consultants will be interested in making sure you can implement project reports, because their reputation is also based on your success.

Don't just look at the consultant's daily rate. Make sure they state the total number of days they are likely to spend on the project and find out what will happen if time overruns. Establish what additional charges there are for any expenses so you can establish an overall project fee.

Set realistic deadlines and insist on regular update meetings. Don't brief a consultant and expect them to go away for a few weeks and come back with the completed work. Much of the value of employing a consultant is in working together to develop suitable solutions and learning from them.

A large proportion of reputable consultants working in the tourism industry are members of the Tourism Society Consultants' Group. You can find details on **www.tourismsociety.org**. The consultants listed have all signed a declaration of good practice.

Additional support
and help

– THE IMPORTANCE OF
TRAINING

– BUSINESS SUPPORT

Working with
consultants

## Chapter 8
# Overseas' marketing

Overseas' visits are increasing and are clearly a very important market, but where do you start? With the whole world as a potential market, overseas' marketing can be daunting – and could be very expensive.

This chapter looks at the value of inbound tourism, targeting the most important markets, how to decide if you are ready to promote to them and how VisitBritain can help.

## A growing and changing market

Inbound tourism is very important to the UK. In 2005, 30 million overseas visitors came, spending £14 billion. The number of inbound visits has been steadily growing, although there have been downturns during difficult times, such as immediately after 9/11 and during the foot-and-mouth outbreak.

The following table shows the top five markets in terms of visits and spend in 2005.

| Country | Visits (000) | Country | Spend (£m) |
| --- | --- | --- | --- |
| USA | 3,438 | USA | 2,384 |
| France | 3,324 | Germany | 998 |
| Germany | 3,294 | Irish Republic | 895 |
| Irish Republic | 2,806 | France | 796 |
| Spain | 1,786 | Spain | 697 |

The average length of stay has been consistently reducing over the last 25 years or so. This is mainly because short breaks have become an increasingly popular option. In addition to leisure visitors, the number of business travellers and people coming to visit their friends and relatives is also increasing.

The countries from which our visitors are drawn are steadily increasing. The low-cost airlines such as Ryanair and easyJet have had a major influence on our inbound tourism markets, creating opportunities for visitors to arrive from an ever-increasing number of new countries. These flights also make good use of less crowded regional airports, so help to disperse inbound visitors throughout the country.

Visitors' expectations have changed. They are increasingly sophisticated and there is a trend towards more independent travel. Britain is perceived as being an expensive destination, so we need to convince visitors of the quality of what we offer.

## Major reasons why visitors come to Britain

These are some of the major reasons why visitors come to Britain:

- **Heritage and History:** historic cities; cathedrals and churches; castles; stately homes and their gardens; archaeological sites; museums and galleries; literary heritage; tradition and pageantry.
- **Countryside and coast:** beauty and diversity of Britain's countryside and coast.
- **Entertainment and the Arts:** the range and quality of Britain's artistic life (in London around 30% of all theatre tickets are bought by overseas visitors); sporting events.
- **Shopping:** range and (sometimes) value for money; designer goods; British-branded goods; street markets.

## Are you ready for overseas' marketing?

Is now a good time for you to start overseas' marketing? It can take time to pay off, so you need to be certain that you have the financial and staffing resources to commit to your chosen markets. Make sure your domestic markets are strong first of all. If you already attract overseas' visitors, you have got a head start.

If you are convinced that overseas' marketing is for you, then draw up a plan of action, using these guidelines.

### 1 WHICH MARKETS WILL YOU FOCUS ON?

Ask yourself who your current customers are and look at where your strongest markets already are. Find out which countries are the key markets for your region. It is going to be easier to attract guests from within those existing markets than starting from scratch.

Consider the strengths of each country. VisitBritain produces market profiles for all their priority markets which you can download free of charge from **www.visitbritain.com/ukindustry**. These essential guides include information on demographics, travel and tourism trends, statistics, and cultural overviews.

If you happen to have an understanding of any of these markets, that is a good place to start. Perhaps there are some language barriers you need to overcome?

### 2 HOW WILL YOU PROMOTE YOUR PRODUCT?

You do not have to go overseas on expensive sales trips to generate business. You can promote using your website, through the tourist boards and third parties such as incoming tour operators.

### 3 THINK ABOUT WHAT YOUR COMPETITORS ARE DOING

Which markets are your competitors targeting? How are you going to position yourself differently? Or perhaps you can see other niche markets where you can be more successful?

### 4 WHAT RESOURCES DO YOU HAVE AVAILABLE?

The costs of launching a product internationally depend greatly on the channels of distribution you have established. You must be prepared to commit substantial effort for three to five years to achieve the full benefit of your investment in overseas' marketing.

**5 TALK TO YOUR NATIONAL OR REGIONAL TOURIST BOARD**
VisitBritain works closely with all national and regional tourist boards to promote Britain as an inbound destination. Your local tourist board should always be your first point of contact when marketing your product. They will be able to advise you on the best potential markets for your particular area.

All tourist boards produce brochures which are distributed to UK and overseas' offices as well as websites. Most offer their members the opportunity to advertise in these. Several tourist boards attend trade and consumer shows, and may be willing to take your brochures, or sub-let some of the stand space to products in their region.

## Working with the travel trade

One way of getting overseas' business without too much expense is to work with handling agents, incoming tour operators and ground handlers who make arrangements for overseas' visitors once they have arrived in the UK. They are based in the UK but promote to overseas' markets. A list of incoming ground handlers, coach and tour operators based in the UK operating in various overseas' markets can be found on the UKinbound website **www.ukinbound.org** (formerly the British Incoming Tour Operators Association).

## How VisitBritain promotes Britain overseas

### OVERSEAS' OFFICES
VisitBritain has limited resources available for promotion, so it naturally has to focus on the strongest markets for Britain. Working with the national tourist boards of England, Scotland and Wales and other major tourism partners, it has identified priority markets and market segments. Key factors to help VisitBritain decide on priority markets include the likely return on investment, potential to generate more out-of-season visitors, and visitors who are likely to travel more widely throughout Britain.

Are you ready for overseas' marketing?

– 1 WHICH MARKETS WILL YOU FOCUS ON?

– 2 HOW WILL YOU PROMOTE YOUR PRODUCT?

– 3 THINK ABOUT WHAT YOUR COMPETITORS ARE DOING

– 4 WHAT RESOURCES DO YOU HAVE AVAILABLE?

– 5 TALK TO YOUR NATIONAL OR REGIONAL TOURIST BOARD

Working with the travel trade

How VisitBritain promotes Britain overseas

– OVERSEAS' OFFICES

– VISITBRITAIN'S FOCUS

– THE 'BRITAIN BRAND'

– WORKING WITH OVERSEAS PRESS

– FREE AND LOW-COST OPPORTUNITIES

## Overseas' marketing checklist

Promoting to overseas' visitors can be a daunting and expensive step. We suggest you use this checklist to make it as cost-effective and easy as possible.

**Consider where your current guests come from**. If you already get quite a few overseas' visitors you're already in a strong position. Try to focus on a maximum of three countries to begin with – you'll find you get guests from other places as well but it makes sense to concentrate your efforts.

**Decide whether to promote directly or through intermediaries.** Do your current overseas' visitors book with you directly or via the web or incoming tour operators or other methods? If you do get bookings through third parties such as tour operators it might be worthwhile contacting others. You can get details of some of them through the UKinbound website *www.ukinbound.org*. If you don't already work with their members, this might be a good place to start.

**Consider which markets are the most important for your area.** You can do this by asking your regional tourist board or speaking to visitor attractions. It is not worth targeting markets that don't already come to the area or those not targeted by your regional tourist board. Partnerships are particularly important for overseas marketing. They help to reduce cost and increase the impact of promotions.

**Find out as much as you can about each of your target markets**. Make sure you read the market profiles on the *www.visitbritain.com/ukindustry* website. Why do visitors from your chosen countries come to Britain? How do they book? When is the best time to promote to them? You'll need to know the answers to these sorts of questions.

continued

How VisitBritain
promotes Britain
overseas

– OVERSEAS' OFFICES

– VISITBRITAIN'S FOCUS

– THE 'BRITAIN BRAND'

– WORKING WITH
OVERSEAS PRESS

– FREE AND LOW-COST
OPPORTUNITIES

**Understand how others promote to overseas' markets.** It's much more cost-effective to undertake joint promotions so make sure you know how your regional tourist board is promoting your area. You could consider advertising in their publications or taking part in a joint sales mission or overseas exhibition.

**Consider whether you need to make any small changes to your service.** For example, you might find that visitors from one of your chosen markets prefer to be allocated twin rooms, or that learning a few welcoming words in their language would help set you above the competition. Try to match the information you provide to the needs and interests of your target markets. If research shows that a nationality has a high propensity for visiting heritage sites, you'll need to highlight which properties are near you and promote your accommodation as a good base from which to see heritage attractions.

**Consider what overseas' marketing you will need to do.** Don't set off on an overseas' sales mission without taking advice from VisitBritain and other experts. Your marketing budget and the size of your accommodation will largely determine how you market your accommodation. If your budget is limited, you can still target overseas' visitors without even leaving the country, by working with tourist boards, incoming tour operators and online.

Here are some potential marketing activities that won't cost the earth.

Update your website so it's clear that you offer a warm welcome to overseas' guests. If you're really serious about overseas' marketing, you might want to set up a micro-site for each target market, translating all the pages so the search engines find your site in each country but this could get expensive. At the very least, you could get a brief welcoming statement or paragraph translated.

continued

> Take advantage of overseas' marketing activities that are already happening. This means you can piggyback on other people's marketing budgets! For example, being quality-assessed means your property is listed on *www.visitbritain.com* and you can participate in joint marketing activities with your regional tourist board.
>
> Consider joining together with visitor attractions and other facilities in your area to offer familiarisation visits for tour operators and overseas' journalists. They are much more likely to feature your area if they know what is on offer.
>
> VisitBritain publishes newsletters for both consumers and the travel trade. Some of these are in E-mail format and others hard copy. Inclusion in some of them is free, so long as you have a strong product and story to tell.
>
> Find out who are the intermediaries for your target markets. In some countries, visitors book mainly through selected tour operators while for others the web is the most important channel.
>
> Direct mail is one of the cheapest ways to promote to overseas' visitors. Make sure you use a recent and targeted mailing list. For example, you might find it most effective to target people with a special interest.

It operates in 35 overseas' markets, including the emerging markets of China, Poland, Russia and South Korea. There are further plans to realise the additional potential in India, Southeast Asia and Eastern Europe.

### VISITBRITAIN'S FOCUS

VisitBritain's marketing has become increasingly focused on the web. The consumer site **www.visitbritain.com** acts as a gateway for different language versions of the site. This network of websites now contains over 50,000 pages of information. More than five million potential visitors have provided their details so they can be sent the latest information on visiting Britain.

VisitBritain still publishes numerous leaflets, guides, maps and magazines for the public and trade. Some publications cover specific themes and campaigns, whereas others focus on particular markets. Recent print campaigns have included activities such as walking, shopping, historic houses and gardens, golf, and themes like 'style and design'.

### THE 'BRITAIN BRAND'

VisitBritain undertook some major research to understand exactly why people come to Britain. From this work it became apparent that tourists are looking for far more than just somewhere they can tick off a list. The research found that visitors wanted an experience and to get close to the people.

Further research then found a way of summing up Britain and capturing the unique spirit of the place and its people. VisitBritain found there are three words that can define Britain as a tourist destination: **depth**, **heart** and **vitality**.

These three words give a real sense of the experience that visitors want: rich in history but with stories to tell; a real warmth and informality of spirit combined with a spark and dynamism that gives Britain its unique sense of pace.

You can learn more about the research and brand essence on **www.visitbritain.org/britainbrand**. The interesting thing about this work is that you can find some elements of your area that you perhaps take for granted but which your guests will find intriguing and appealing.

### WORKING WITH OVERSEAS' PRESS

It is possible to develop your own overseas' media contacts and to build relationships with them, but this could be time-consuming and expensive. By working with the VisitBritain Press Office you will potentially have access to many more contacts. VisitBritain provides regular feature articles, news stories and photographs to over 1,000 overseas' newspapers, magazines and correspondents, so it is worthwhile sending your press information to VisitBritain Press Office for possible inclusion.

How VisitBritain promotes Britain overseas

- OVERSEAS' OFFICES
- VISITBRITAIN'S FOCUS
- THE 'BRITAIN BRAND'
- WORKING WITH OVERSEAS' PRESS
- FREE AND LOW-COST OPPORTUNITIES

Press visits are another important aspect of their activities targeting the media. Journalists from the press, radio and television are invited to experience different aspects of Britain first-hand. Some journalists visit as part of a general promotion or on themed itineraries, such as one covering the arts or gardens.

Journalists are drawn from daily newspapers with mass readership, glossy monthly magazines and appropriate special-interest publications. Broadcast media, which plays an increasingly important role in VisitBritain's worldwide publicity, has the potential to access huge audiences and to generate publicity worth millions of pounds.

The Press and PR Department at VisitBritain in London coordinates the programme with assistance from its overseas' offices. Publications, broadcast programmes and freelance journalists are carefully targeted under a 12-month media plan designed to address the needs of each market.

Once a journalist has accepted an invitation to travel to Britain, programmes are developed according to their needs. They are always on the lookout for good-quality accommodation for journalists to enjoy. If asked to participate in the hosting of a media visit, you will receive full details of the relevant publication/broadcast, its circulation/viewing figures and the journalist's story objectives. In return you will need to provide free accommodation.

The overseas' PR managers send copies of all stories and broadcasts to VisitBritain's London office. Accommodation providers who are mentioned are sent a copy of the story. If you are interested in hosting international press visits, contact the International Press Visits team at VisitBritain.

### FREE AND LOW-COST OPPORTUNITIES

VisitBritain offers a wide range of opportunities which are either low cost or even free of charge.

Accommodation providers can obtain a free entry on **www.visitbritain.com** or **www.enjoyengland.com**

accommodation providers, provided you have been quality assessed by one of the recognised inspection bodies.

You can also obtain free editorial in the UK Product and Destination Update distributed to all VisitBritain travel trade staff, who then use the copy in their own newsletters sent to their local travel trade database.

VisitBritain also organises a programme of familiarisation visits for tour operators and travel agents so they can gain more detailed information about different aspects of Britain. Each programme is different and may cover specific themes or regions. If you would like to be considered for inclusion in a familiarisation visit, you will need to offer complimentary services or heavily discounted rates. Similar opportunities exist for press familiarisation visits when VisitBritain hosts journalists from overseas.

VisitBritain also organises overseas workshops and sales missions, offering an opportunity to make direct contacts with the travel trade. The workshops and sales missions are useful for the first venture into a new market, and need to be followed up with individual sales activities and direct mail to maintain contact.

You can search all VisitBritain's marketing opportunities within the trade website **www.visitbritain.com/ukindustry**.

How VisitBritain
promotes Britain
overseas

- OVERSEAS' OFFICES
- VISITBRITAIN'S FOCUS
- THE 'BRITAIN BRAND'
- WORKING WITH
  OVERSEAS' PRESS
- FREE AND LOW-COST
  OPPORTUNITIES

# Chapter 9

# Higher quality for higher profits

When visitors are away from home, they want to be certain that wherever they stay, it will be comfortable and high quality. They want to know what to expect, and that their precious holiday time and money are going to be well spent.

Telling visitors that you have a good-quality product is one thing, but being able to say that an independent assessor thinks so is quite another. A quality assurance rating is a mark of quality that is both nationally and internationally recognised. It tells your potential guests that you have pride in what you do and want to provide the highest standards possible. With increased competition, it makes sense to take advantage of any opportunity to stand out and reassure customers.

## New harmonised standards

VisitBritain, VisitScotland and VisitWales have agreed new common standards across the accommodation sectors (including serviced accommodation, self-catering properties and hostels) which are now being rolled out progressively. The Automobile Association (AA) has also agreed to deliver common standards with VisitBritain, VisitScotland and VisitWales for the service sector, such as hotels, bed and breakfasts and guest houses.

## Promoting only quality-assessed accommodation

From 1st January 2006, VisitBritain will only promote quality-assessed accommodation through its full range of marketing activity. Properties can be quality assessed by VisitBritain, VisitScotland, VisitWales or the AA. This policy has the full backing of the Department for Culture, Media and Sport and is already applied by many of the English regions and local authorities, as well as by VisitWales and VisitScotland.

## The family of Quality Assurance Schemes

VisitBritain now has a Quality Assurance Scheme for all forms of accommodation:

- **Hotels** (star rating): usually larger serviced establishments offering a defined set of services and facilities. Town houses, country house hotels and travel accommodation also have defined standards within this scheme.
- **Guest accommodation** (diamond rating – moving to stars in 2006–7): usually smaller serviced establishments including guest houses, B&Bs, farmhouses and inns.
- **Hostels** (star rating): serviced and/or self-catering accommodation in hostels, backpacker's hotels and camping barns.
- **Self-catering** (star rating): cottages, houses, flats and apartments.
- **Holiday parks** (star rating): caravan, camping, touring and chalet parks.
- **Holiday villages** (star rating): as for holiday parks, but also offering extensive leisure facilities, food outlets, leisure activities and entertainment.
- **Campus accommodation** (star rating): serviced and self-catering accommodation offered by universities and colleges.
- **Restaurants with rooms**: for businesses that are first and foremost a high-quality restaurant, but with some accommodation available.

New harmonised standards

Promoting only quality-assessed accommodation

The family of Quality Assurance Schemes

- **National Accessible Scheme**: a rating for establishments that can meet defined criteria to assist visitors with mobility, hearing and visual impairments.
- **Walkers Welcome and Cyclists Welcome**: two new schemes that can be used in addition to the Quality Assurance rating to show that the accommodation provider offers special facilities and services for the benefit of walkers and cyclists.

## Summary of the standards for each type of accommodation

### HOTEL ACCOMMODATION
Hotels are divided into three categories:

*Hotel*
- Formal accommodation with full service.
- Likely to have in excess of 20 guest bedrooms.
- **Country house hotel**: a country house with ample grounds or gardens, in a rural or semi-rural situation. Emphasis on peace and quiet.
- **Small hotel**: hotel with a maximum of 20 guest bedrooms. Personally run by the proprietor and likely to have limited business function.

*Town house hotel*
- High-quality town/city centre properties of individual and distinctive style, with a maximum of 50 guest bedrooms.
- High staff-to-guest ratio.
- Public areas may be limited.
- Possibly no restaurant, but room service available instead.

*Metro hotel*
- A town/city hotel providing full hotel services with the exception of dinner.
- A range of places to eat will be within easy walking distance.

Hotels are given a rating from one to five stars: the more stars, the higher the quality and the greater the range of facilities and level of services provided.

*One star*

- Tend to be smaller properties, privately owned and open seven days a week during operating season.
- Simple, practical style accommodation with a limited range of facilities and services.
- All bedrooms will have en-suite or private bath/shower rooms.
- Dining room/restaurant or similar eating area serving a cooked breakfast seven days a week (except some designated town house hotels) and evening meals at least five days a week (except some designated town house hotels and metro hotels).
- Licensed bar or lounge.
- Friendly and courteous staff offering efficient if limited levels of service.

*Two stars*

- Tend to be smaller privately owned properties, resort and small commercial hotels.
- Well-presented accommodation offering a fair degree of space and convenience.
- Décor and furnishings may be simple but well maintained.
- Evening meals will be available seven days a week in a dining room/restaurant or similar eating area.
- Services may be limited but efficient, provided by proprietor, management or well-trained staff.

*Three stars*

- A higher percentage of group-style hotels will fall into this category, together with many high-quality privately owned properties.
- More formal style of hotel, likely to be larger with greater range of facilities and services.
- Bedroom accommodation will be more spacious and designed for comfort and convenient use, for example, writing desk/dressing table.

- Service will be relatively formal, with a staffed reception desk.
- Access will be available 24 hours a day.
- Lounge/bar and room service serving hot and cold drinks and light snacks during daytime and evening.
- Provision of at least one room-service meal, either continental breakfast or dinner.

*Four stars*

- Usually larger, group-style hotels where more formal levels of service would be expected.
- Accommodation of a very high standard, offering a wide range of facilities and services, with quality to match.
- All bedrooms will be designed and furnished for comfort and ease of use, with very good quality furniture, beds and soft furnishings.
- All rooms en-suite, with at least half offering a bath in addition to shower facilities.
- At least one suite available.
- Service will reflect the same quality and attention to detail.
- Access all day and night, facilitated by on-duty staff.
- Formal reception and porters' desks with uniformed staff offering a proactive style of service.
- Catering standards will reflect a serious approach to food and drink, with table service provided in bar and/or lounge.
- At least one restaurant, open to residents and non-residents, for breakfast and dinner seven days a week.
- 24-hour room service including cooked breakfast, main meals and lighter snacks and beverages.

*Five stars*

- Accommodation of a luxury quality with services to match.
- Spacious bedrooms, suites and public areas.
- Selection of catering options all offering cuisine and service of the highest international quality.
- Open seven days a week, all year.

- All bedrooms with en-suite bathroom, with bath and thermostatically controlled shower.
- A number of permanent luxury suites available. At least one restaurant open to residents and non-residents for all meals seven days a week.
- Enhanced services offered, for example, valet parking, 24-hour reception and room service, concierge service, proactive table service in bars, lounges and at breakfast, full afternoon tea.
- Additional facilities available, for example, secondary dining, leisure, business centre, spa, retail, etc.
- Highly trained, professional staff providing exceptional levels of anticipatory service.

*Gold and silver awards*
- These are awarded to properties that not only achieve their overall rating, but also exceed the expectations within their rating level. The awards recognise the high level of comfort, cleanliness, hospitality and service afforded.
- **Silver**: this award recognises high quality in all areas of the business, with very good levels of customer care.
- **Gold**: properties achieving a Gold award will demonstrate exceptional levels of quality, comfort, cleanliness, hospitality and attentive service.

## OTHER SERVICED ACCOMMODATION
*Bed and breakfasts*
- Accommodation provided in a private house, run by the owner and with no more than six paying guests.

*Guest house*
- Accommodation provided for more than six paying guests and run on a more commercial basis than a B&B.
- Usually more services, for example, dinner, provided by staff as well as the owner.

*Farmhouse*
- B&B or guest house accommodation provided on a working farm or smallholding.

*Inn*

- Accommodation provided in a fully licensed establishment. The bar will be open to non-residents and provide food in the evenings.

*Restaurant with rooms*

- Destination restaurant offering overnight accommodation with the restaurant being the main business, open to non-residents.
- The restaurant will offer a high standard of food and service at least five nights a week.
- The establishment will have a liquor licence and a maximum of 12 guest bedrooms.

*Guest accommodation*

- Any establishment that meets the minimum requirements can be designated in this general sub-category.
- Establishments are given a rating from one to five stars: the more stars, the higher the quality, and the greater the range of facilities and level of services provided. The same minimum requirements apply to all categories.

*One star*

- Simple, no-frills accommodation suitable for those on a tighter budget.
- Décor will be clean and furnishings fit for purpose.
- Beds will be made up with clean linen and bedding; towels and fresh soap provided.
- Bedrooms will have a form of heating, acceptable lighting levels and privacy.
- Bathroom facilities may be shared and hot water will be available at reasonable times.
- As a minimum, breakfast will be provided – either a full cooked meal or, if advertised in advance, a substantial continental breakfast.
- Service levels may be limited.

*Two stars*

- Accommodation offering a good overall level of quality together with some facility and service enhancements, for example, in-room televisions, fitted heating.

- Décor will be in good condition, the furniture sound and lighting well positioned.
- Flooring will provide adequate comfort underfoot.
- Bath or shower rooms may be en-suite or shared with other guests and/or proprietor, facilities being maintained in a clean and serviceable condition.
- Additional services may be provided, for example, dinner. Meals may be simple with limited choice, but will be freshly prepared.

*Three stars*

- A good level of quality in all areas.
- Bedrooms will offer a reasonable amount of space and comfort, for example, access to both sides of double beds.
- Décor will show elements of coordination with the soft furnishings.
- Furniture will be more substantial and may provide additional facilities, for example, writing desk.
- Conveniently positioned lighting and controllable heating.
- En-suite facilities, where provided, may be compact but will be clean and well maintained.
- Toiletries (e.g. shampoo, shower gel) are likely to be provided.
- All rooms will have a washbasin facility.
- A greater selection of items may be offered at breakfast, including choice of eggs cooked to order.
- Service throughout will be efficient and hospitable.

*Four stars*

- Very good quality in all areas.
- Bedrooms will be more spacious with greater emphasis on quality of décor, furnishings, fixtures and fittings.
- Extra facilities and personal touches may be provided, for example, hairdryer, radio.
- At least half the bedrooms will have en-suite facilities, which will be well fitted with quality sanitaryware, effective lighting and ventilation.
- Towels will be of a high quality and a range of toiletries will be provided.

Summary of the standards for each type of accommodation

– HOTEL ACCOMMODATION

– OTHER SERVICED ACCOMMODATION

– SELF-CATERING ACCOMMODATION

- A very good breakfast will be offered, with a wide selection of starter and cooked options.
- Local or homemade specialities may be featured, with an emphasis on fresh ingredients.
- Service and guest care will be attentive, efficient and hospitable.

*Five stars*
- Excellent quality accommodation with exceptional levels of hospitality.
- Bedrooms will offer ample space with excellent comfort and elements of luxury.
- High quality décor, furnishings and fittings will feature in all guest areas.
- All bedrooms will be en-suite or have private facilities, which will be fitted out with high-quality sanitaryware and fixtures.
- Luxury towelling, including bath sheets and a wide range of quality toiletries.
- Public areas will offer the same high quality as the bedrooms and provide guests with additional space for comfort and relaxation.
- Breakfast will offer a wide selection of produce, such as freshly squeezed fruit juices, fruits in season, bakery items and homemade preserves.
- Cooked options will be numerous, possibly with some original or regional specialities.
- Service and hospitality levels will be exemplary.

*Gold and silver awards*
- These are awarded to properties that not only achieve their overall rating, but also exceed the expectations within their rating level. The awards recognise the high level of comfort, cleanliness, hospitality and service afforded.
- **Silver**: this award recognises high quality in all areas of the business, with very good levels of customer care.
- **Gold**: properties achieving a Gold award will demonstrate exceptional levels of quality, comfort, cleanliness, hospitality and attentive service.

SELF-CATERING ACCOMMODATION

Minimum entry requirements include the following:

- High standard of cleanliness throughout.
- Pricing and conditions of booking made clear.
- Local information to help you make the best of your stay.
- Comfortable accommodation with a range of furniture to meet your needs.
- Colour television (where signal available) at no extra charge.
- Kitchen equipped to meet all essential requirements.

Serviced apartments provide self-catering accommodation with additional elements of service, for example, 24-hour concierge service, five out of seven days cleaning service.

*One star*

- Simple style accommodation, where all areas are safe and clean.
- Unlikely to be self-contained (e.g. might have a shared bathroom).
- All equipment provided will work and be fit for its purpose. The accommodation will be cleaned for guests' arrival.
- Beds of at least standard adult size (unless advertised otherwise), provided with clean bedding in sufficient quantity. Linen may or may not be provided.
- Potential visitors will be given advance details of accommodation, facilities and services available.
- Health, Safety and Statutory obligations complied with.

*Two stars*

- All units will be self-contained.
- Generally good overall quality of décor, furnishings and fixtures, which may be of a practical or older style.
- Space may be limited, particularly in bedrooms.
- At least one bathroom and WC for up to eight guests.
- Limited additional facilities and services.

*Three stars*

- Quality of décor and furnishings will demonstrate greater attention to coordination and practicality.

Summary of the standards for each type of accommodation

- HOTEL ACCOMMODATION

  OTHER SERVICED ACCOMMODATION

- SELF-CATERING ACCOMMODATION

- More spacious accommodation offering greater levels of comfort and freedom of movement, for example, access to both sides of double beds.
- Good lighting provision, with each occupant provided with bedside table and lamp.
- Controlled heating.
- Wider range of appliances, including microwave oven and access to vacuum cleaner.
- Some leisure facilities, for example, boxed games, toys, barbecue, as appropriate.

*Four stars*

- Comfortable accommodation, decorated to a high standard.
- Usually more spacious with very good quality furniture, soft furnishings, beds and floorings.
- Bedlinen and towels provided, with or without an additional charge.
- More extensive range of appliances, including access to washing machine and tumble dryer (or 24-hour laundry service).
- Additional separate WC available if more than six guests can be accommodated.
- Additional facilities, for example, leisure, may be provided.
- All equipment and facilities in good order.

*Five stars*

- Excellent quality accommodation, demonstrating the best of its type available.
- A high specification evident in all areas.
- Attention to detail shown in design, both internal and external, with exemplary standards of care and maintenance.
- Sleeping in designated bedrooms only, in other words, no sofa beds.
- Full range of appliances and equipment including freezer, dishwasher, in-house laundry facilities (or 24-hour service) and video/DVD player.
- Telephone provided, capable of receiving incoming and making outgoing calls.

## Case study

*View from a hotelier*

*Raffles Hotel in Blackpool invests around £275 annually to join VisitBritain's national Quality Assurance Standards. This covers assessors' visits and inclusion in the* Where to Stay Guide *and consumer website. Raffles received a 4-diamond rating.*

*Here is what the owner-manager says about it.*

'One of the best things about the scheme is that we get a truly independent view of the hotel. The assessors check all aspects of the guest's stay, noticing things that we wouldn't ordinarily pick up on. Their style is one of encouragement, and they've given us some great marketing ideas and helped to get Raffles on the conference delegate circuit.

Because of our 4-diamond status they suggested we increase our rates. This worried us initially. But we've found that customers are prepared to pay that little bit extra to be assured of quality, especially in the high season when supply outstrips demand.

Our occupancy now runs at 87%. Knowing an assessor could call unannounced at any time helps to keep us on our toes!

Raffles was named in *The Guardian* as one of the 50 best small hotels in England. It has 17 en-suite bedrooms and two large suites and very popular traditional tea rooms.'

**Graham Poole, Joint owner-manager of Raffles Hotel, Blackpool**

Summary of the standards for each type of accommodation

- HOTEL ACCOMMODATION

- OTHER SERVICED ACCOMMODATION

- SELF-CATERING ACCOMMODATION

- Bedlinen and towels available and included in charge.
- Extra bath or shower, WC and washbasin provided if more than six guests can be accommodated.
- Where leisure facilities are provided these will be in excellent order, under supervision where appropriate and with extended opening hours to suit customer needs.
- Management organisation and levels of guest care will be exemplary.

## Benefits of assessment in promotional terms

The process for becoming quality assessed is straightforward. After submission of the application, an assessor is assigned to the property. Their visit is booked and then the assessment is completed. Feedback is given to the proprietor. A written report and certificate are then sent to the proprietor confirming the rating.

The assessor usually offers feedback about services and can give guidance on potential improvements. They will usually talk to you about how you can improve your rating, or about better ways to define your market and how to let your quality rating guide your pricing.

VisitBritain and EnjoyEngland are investing in marketing and public relations' activities to increase public awareness of and demand for assured products and visitor experiences.

Other promotional benefits include:

- free promotion in the VisitBritain *Where to Stay Guides*, which generate over three million enquiries per year;
- free promotion with a detailed listing and photography on the VisitBritain and EnjoyEngland websites, which attract over 28 million visitors – generating over 300,000 direct bookings for the English tourism industry;
- free promotion to over 4.5 million customers throughout the world via VisitBritain's 300 or more marketing campaigns;
- free promotion exclusively to more than 560 Tourist Information Centres throughout England, who make in excess of 275,000 bookings per year;

- free Quality in Tourism sign to all new participants to promote your rating;
- free use of the Quality in Tourism logo – the industry leader in quality standards – on your signage, letterheads and other stationery.

## Further information

You can obtain full details about the quality standards on **www.qualityintourism.com**.

# Chapter 10
# Accessibility

There are around ten million disabled people in the UK. If you add to this figure the friends and families who are likely to travel with them, you can quickly see how huge this market is. It makes economic sense to be aware of the needs of disabled people as well as now being the law. The Disability Discrimination Act (DDA) has been introduced in three stages and it is now essential that you comply with this law.

This chapter explains the scope of the DDA and suggests some steps you could take to ensure you comply with it and are able to access this important market.

## What the Disability Discrimination Act says

The Disability Discrimination Act was introduced in three stages. All of these stages are now in full force so you need to comply with all of them. In 1996, it became unlawful to refuse to serve a disabled person, or to offer them a different or inferior service. Since 1999, service providers have had to consider making reasonable adjustments to the way they deliver their services so that disabled people can use them. It should be noted that 'service' can include information as well as physical services.

Since October 2004, service providers may have to consider making permanent changes to premises, where physical features make access to their services impossible or unreasonably difficult for disabled people.

'Service providers' include restaurants, hotels and other forms of accommodation.

What the Disability Discrimination Act says

Providing better access to services is not just about installing ramps and widening doorways for wheelchair users. It is about making services easier to use for all disabled people, including people who are blind, deaf or have a learning disability.

A disability is defined as 'a physical or mental impairment which has a substantial and long-term adverse effect on his/her ability to carry out normal day-to-day activities'. Based on this definition, it is easy to see why the accumulated spending power of the UK disabled market is over £45 billion points per annum.

You probably know people with a disability, not just those in wheelchairs, but with long-term conditions such as diabetes or asthma. It is important to note though that not everyone with a disability considers themselves to be disabled.

The law states that failure to make reasonable adjustments without justification is discrimination. Examples of reasonable adjustments could include:

- installing an induction loop for people who are hearing-impaired
- giving the option to book tickets by E-mail as well as by phone
- providing disability awareness training for staff who have contact with the public.
- providing larger, well-defined signage for people with impaired vision
- putting in a ramp at the entrance to a building instead of, or as well as, steps.

## Making reasonable adjustments

Making reasonable adjustments

What is considered a 'reasonable adjustment' for a large organisation like a chain hotel may be different to a reasonable adjustment for a small guest house. It is about what is practical in each individual situation, and the resources of the business. You are not required to make changes which are impractical or beyond your means.

Failure or refusal to provide a service that is offered to other people to a disabled person is taken to be discriminatory unless it can be justified.

The word 'reasonable' is important as it does not necessarily mean you have to remove the feature if this is very difficult or costly for you. You can also:

- alter the feature so it is no longer so difficult
- suggest a way of avoiding it
- provide another way of making your services accessible.

## Dealing with disabled people

Some people are nervous of speaking to disabled people or dealing with them because they are scared of saying 'the wrong thing'. Part of the reason for this is that they recognise that there are some politically correct phrases which it might be better to use, but are not quite sure what they are.

Don't use generic labels for groups of disabled people, such as 'the blind' or 'the disabled'. Try to emphasise the person and not the impairment, and say things like 'person who is deaf' or 'disabled people' instead. Say things like 'children who are blind' rather than 'blind children'.

The most important thing to remember is that you are dealing with people with disabilities. If you were to suddenly become disabled, you would still be the same person, and continue to think of yourself as an individual who probably does not like to be 'lumped together' into a pot or described in a stereotypical way.

A group of people may be blind, and have similar physical needs related to their disability, but their mindsets and attitudes to life will still be different. Disabled people are individuals, just like you. So any generalisation is difficult.

## Helping people with visual impairments

Making reasonable
adjustments

There are many simple physical improvements that everyone can make without spending a fortune. Here are just some of them:

Dealing with disabled
people

- Have at least one copy of information in large print.
- Accept working or service dogs.

Helping people with
visual impairments

- Use clear typefaces, contrasting colours and non-reflective signs. Ensure they are well lit. If you use Braille signs, make sure they are at the right height.
- If someone looks as if they need assistance, offer it, but wait for them to accept before you help. Speak to people with visual impairments before you take their arm. Tell them what you are planning to do as you guide them around, giving clear instructions and explanations such as 'We're about to go up three deep steps.'

## Helping people with hearing difficulties

Helping people with
hearing difficulties

- Have writing materials handy for people with hearing difficulties.
- Try to speak to anyone with hearing difficulties in a place away from too many other sounds. Move away from a TV lounge (or switch off the TV).
- Ensure that you and your staff speak clearly, and look straight at customers so they can lip-read if they wish.
- Consider installing an induction loop to help people with hearing aids hear more clearly.
- Many people (up to half a million) find it difficult to use a conventional telephone. Offer alternative ways of communicating such as fax or E-mail. Many people with hearing difficulties use text on their mobile phone, even when standing next to the person they are 'speaking' to.
- Could you or your staff enrol on a British Sign Language course? Even if you can only learn the basics, this might be very helpful to some of your customers.

## Helping people who have physical disabilities or problems with mobility

- Make a low desk available for reception, or ensure that reception staff approach a wheelchair user and do not lean over the desk.
- Talk directly to the disabled person, not their carer.
- When talking to a wheelchair user, do not lean on the wheelchair or invade their personal space.
- When promoting your accommodation, make sure you provide full information on how accessible it is. It is frustrating for people when they are given the wrong information. It is best to give full and accurate descriptions (for example, entrance has one step, seven inches high) so that individuals can decide on whether your building is accessible to them, rather than you trying to make a decision on their behalf.

## Making promotional material more accessible

Around 2 million people in UK are blind or partially sighted. This figure does not include those who have temporary sight disturbances for whatever reason, or some older (and younger!) people who simply appreciate easy-to-read information. There are several ways of providing information for people who are blind or have only partial sight:

- You can provide information in Braille, but do not assume everyone can read Braille – many people would prefer large print.
- Offer 'large' print – this usually means a font size between 16 and 22 points.
- Provide 'clear' print by following the guidelines below. This simply means making your print material clear and easy to read, so it is good practice for everyone and not just targeting people with visual impairments.
- Use a minimum font size of 12 (The Royal National Institute for the Blind recommend 14).
- Strong contrast aids legibility, for example, dark text on a light background. Reversed-out text is very hard to read

(e.g. white text on a black background). Red can also be hard to read.

- Use straightforward typefaces and avoid ornate ones or simulated handwriting.
- Keep plenty of space between lines – 1.5 – double-spaced text.
- Bold type is easier to read for many people. Clusters of capital letters can be hard.
- Make numbers distinctive – 3, 5, 8 and 0 are easily confused.
- Short sentences and paragraphs are easier to read (for everyone).
- Don't condense or stretch lines of text.
- Align text to left margin. This is because some special reading software for people with visual impairments needs a definite left-hand margin in order to work properly.
- Avoid justified text as large gaps can be confusing.
- Don't set type over images. This has become fashionable in design terms, but can be confusing for everyone.
- Glare can make glossy paper harder to read.
- Avoid thin paper – where type shows through from the other side.

## Promoting your accessible facilities

Unfortunately, not enough places offer good and accessible facilities. If you can do so, that is great, because you will be able to attract new visitors and generate good publicity for your company.

Here are a few other ways to let people know what you offer:

- Buy or source mailing lists of people belonging to particular organisations, or try to find lists with a higher proportion of older people who might be interested in your services.
- Target all the relevant publications and media for the disabilities you can cater for. Don't forget 'talking newspapers' (**www.tnauk.org.uk**) to target people with visual impairments. Local radio stations are also a good

Helping people who have physical disabilities or problems with mobility

Making promotional material more accessible

Promoting your accessible facilities

way to reach them, as are newspapers such as *Disability Now*.

- There are some guidebooks that specifically deal with holidays for disabled people, such as RADAR's *Holidays in Britain and Ireland*.
- Some websites like **www.youreable.com** have good communities of disabled people. There are websites targeting people with practically every disability you can think of.
- Invite journalists and members of disability groups to come and try out your services for themselves. Word of mouth is a very important source of new business for many communities.
- Make sure local Tourist Information Centres are fully aware of how accessible your services are.

## National Accessible Scheme

The National Accessible Scheme for self-catering, parks and serviced accommodation includes standards for hearing and visually impaired guests, in addition to standards for guests with mobility impairment.

Accommodation is thoroughly assessed and then allowed to display one of the following symbols, so that disabled people and their carers will know what level of facility and service they can expect.

MOBILITY

Promoting your
accessible facilities

National Accessible
Scheme
- MOBILITY
- HEARING IMPAIRMENT
- VISUAL IMPAIRMENT

**Level 1 (M1):** typically suitable for a person with sufficient mobility to climb a flight of steps, but would benefit from fixtures and fittings to aid balance.

**Level 2 (M2):** typically suitable for a person with restricted walking ability, and for those who may need to use a wheelchair some of the time and can negotiate a maximum of three steps.

**Level 3 (M3-I) Independent:** typically suitable for a person who depends on the use of a wheelchair, and transfers unaided to and from the wheelchair in a seated position. This person may be an independent traveller.

**Level 3 (M3-A) Assisted:** typically suitable for a person who depends on the use of a wheelchair in a seated position. This person also requires personal/mechanical assistance (e.g. carer, hoist).

**Access Exceptional:** attained by providing for all levels of mobility impairment listed above with reference to the British Standards BS 8300:2001. This is awarded to establishments that fulfil all the requirements of M1, M2, M3 (A or I) and some additional Best Practice criteria.

HEARING IMPAIRMENT

**Level 1 (H1):** minimum entry requirements to meet the National Accessible Standards for guests with hearing impairment, from mild hearing loss to profoundly deaf.

**Level 2 (H2):** recommended (Best Practice) additional requirements to meet the National Accessible Standards for guests with hearing impairment, from mild hearing loss to profoundly deaf.

VISUAL IMPAIRMENT

**Level 1 (V1):** minimum entry requirement to meet the National Accessible Standards for visually impaired guests.

**Level 2 (V2):** recommended (Best Practice) additional requirements to meet the National Accessible Standards for visually impaired guests.

## Further information

**www.disability.gov.uk**   Official government site for disability matters
**www.drc-gb.org**   Disability Rights Commission
**www.radar.org.uk**   The Disability network
**www.holidaycare.org.uk**   Holiday Care Service
**www.tourismforall.org.uk**   Tourism for All
**www.rnib.org.uk**   Royal National Institute of the Blind
**www.rnid.org.uk**   RNID – representing the deaf and hard of hearing

National Accessible
Scheme

– MOBILITY
– HEARING IMPAIRMENT
– VISUAL IMPAIRMENT

Further information

# Chapter 11
# Coping with the unexpected

At some stage it is likely that you might have to cope with the unexpected and have some form of crisis to manage. In recent years we have experienced the effects of foot-and-mouth disease, 9/11 and the London bombings. Most companies have learnt to their cost that if they are not prepared when disaster hits, their business will suffer.

We hope you will never need this chapter, but if you read it, it will help you plan in advance for any negative eventuality. Your business will recover quickly if you are prepared for the worst.

## Frontline staff

In a crisis you and your staff are probably the most important aspect of your business. You and your staff are the frontline and can reassure guests and stop you from losing further business. At the same time, your staff may be feeling nervous about the situation, so it is best to keep them fully involved and informed so they do not pass on their worries to the public. Keeping staff calm and motivated, and helping them to take important decisions on their own when necessary is important.

Make sure you keep staff lists, including mobile phone numbers, updated so you know how to contact people in an emergency. Build in regular briefings to staff so you can give them the latest information and listen to anything they have picked up from guests or potential guests.

Once the crisis is over, make sure you recognise the contribution of any staff who coped particularly well.

Frontline staff

## Dealing with guests in a crisis

Dealing with guests in a crisis
– TRAVEL ADVISORIES
– CANCELLATIONS

Depending on the crisis, guests will worry about their safety and want to have the latest information. You will get cancellations and possibly negative comments. You cannot anticipate every potential problem in advance, but you can prepare the sort of information you are likely to need.

### TRAVEL ADVISORIES
In the event of an emergency or crisis situation governments usually issue advice to their residents, often through a Foreign Office or equivalent. In the UK you would be able to see the government's advice on the Foreign and Commonwealth Office website.

Travellers do take note of the travel advisories issued by their government, partly because these are usually picked up by the media and widely distributed. Insurance companies also judge whether to pay claims based on travel advisories, so it is useful to know what advice has been given. Bear in mind that the advice may be updated and changed quite frequently so you will need to keep informed.

### CANCELLATIONS
It is likely that you will have to deal with some cancellations. Customers might feel their safety is at risk or the situation means that they will not be able to do all the things they expected. All accommodation providers need to have a cancellation policy in place and to make this part of the booking process. You can only apply your cancellation policy if it is made clear at the time of booking. This then means that if the guest refuses to pay you may be able to charge the amount against their credit card.

You need to advise guests at the time of booking that their card will be charged in the event of cancellation. If you have a written statement to this effect or brief script for reservation staff, you will be able to prove to the credit card company that you are abiding by a fair policy.

In the event of a crisis situation, if your accommodation is still open for business then your contract with a guest is still binding. However, in certain situations your accommodation may remain open but other facilities could be restricted. In this case the contract is considered to be 'frustrated'. This means that if a guest wishes to cancel they can and any deposit will need to be repaid. However, you would be able to deduct any expenses such as advance purchase of food.

When a guest cancels a firm booking (where they have agreed to your cancellation policy when they made that booking) without such cause they are in breach of contract. You can make a claim if you have made every attempt to re-let their room at the same price and failed to do so. You can claim the value of the booking less any expenses that you have not needed to incur, such as food.

If you cancel the booking then you are in breach of the contract and the guest is entitled to claim damages from you to compensate them for any loss. Sometimes guests may be willing to accept credit notes against a future stay instead of a direct refund. The advantage of this is that the cash is kept in the business.

Please note that this information should be used as a guideline only. You are strongly advised to take legal advice when drafting cancellation policies. VisitBritain's Pink Guide is a very useful source of information about legislation relating to accommodation providers.

## Providing good-quality information

It is natural to be most concerned about immediate bookings, but you also need to protect those in the near future. Guests who plan to stay with you at some point in the next few weeks may be nervous and have some concerns about honouring their booking, although they may not actually bother to contact you.

You need to develop a 'business as usual' attitude which is credible, reassuring and still takes account of possible concerns. Imagine what anxieties you might have if you were a potential guest at your accommodation, and set out to find solutions or responses to those concerns.

It is a good idea to list some of the possible worries and to find a way to counteract each of them. You can then draw up a 'business as usual' statement or letter which staff can use to respond to enquiries and problems, and which you can send out to people who have made bookings for the coming weeks. Don't deny that this is a difficult situation, but find ways of mitigating it and if possible, demonstrate that it is not as bad as might initially be thought.

You might be able to find some small treat, arrange access to an unusual attraction or do something for guests to show you appreciate their continued custom and to give them something positive to talk about when they go home. Remember that at times like this, word-of-mouth publicity becomes even more important.

It is usually a good idea to meet with your tourist board and other local businesses to discuss your responses and look at how you can work together to overcome any difficulties.

Make sure you have a consistent response to any enquiries and ensure your website always has the latest, most up-to-date and accurate information on it. You might also like to include additional links to other reassuring sources of information.

## Maintaining good relationships with the media

If you have been undertaking any PR activities, your media contacts will be invaluable. When there is a crisis, there are usually two stages to the media reaction. At first you will probably find that most stories are negative and mainly consist of an element of scaremongering and outrage. The media look for examples of the damage that has been done, the amount of business lost and the effects of this.

After a little while, you will start to notice some more positive stories amongst the gloom. There is often a sense of emerging from the disaster, rallying round and fighting back. At this stage the media are more ready for brief success

Dealing with guests in a crisis

&ndash; TRAVEL ADVISORIES

&ndash; CANCELLATIONS

Providing good-quality information

Maintaining good relationships with the media

stories or quirky examples of how some businesses are overcoming adversity.

As part of your PR planning you should think about how you will deal with any crisis situation. Think about the person who is most likely to be able to handle any media enquiries. This should be someone who is confident and able to answer questions calmly and succinctly. It is a good idea to think in advance about any likely questions and how you will answer them. Prepare a list of your official responses to key questions so staff will all have a ready and consistent answer.

Check also what other organisations such as your tourist board are saying. Sometimes you can raise your profile by standing out and making a different statement to the mainstream one, but you should only do this if you are very certain of your situation and confident you are not doing any damage.

At the more optimistic stage of media communications, you might find you can generate some useful press coverage for your business. Perhaps you can show that you are forging ahead with new marketing ideas and making the best of the situation.

## Marketing

When faced with a reduction in their business, the first reaction of many accommodation providers is to panic. The second is to discount in order to attract more guests as soon as possible. This might work and generate some additional business, but there are several downsides to consider.

Firstly of course there is the reduced revenue. You might get more guests, but if the rates they are paying are low the actual profit may not be worth the effort and wear and tear on your building, unless secondary spend is good. After prolonged periods of discounts, there is also a tendency for the public to think that it is the normal price. Discounting also means that you are putting out a message that you really need business – and that is not always a good thing. More guests will be attracted by a confident attitude.

It is far better to think about the main reasons why guests may not want to come, analyse the potential barriers and look at how you might overcome them. You can think up a compelling call to action without necessarily cutting prices, although discounts may be useful.

There are several other marketing tactics that you can consider when you need to cope with the unexpected.

### POSTPONE YOUR MARKETING
Although it is tempting to place new advertising immediately to try to generate more business, the best policy is often to wait a week or two. There is no point in spending precious marketing budgets unless you know it will reap good returns. You also need to ensure that any planned advertising still has an appropriate message. It is usually better to batten down the hatches and keep promotional spend to a minimum for a week or so. Spend time rather than money so you are confident that you have planned what to do and your budget will be invested more wisely.

### ADDED VALUE
If you still feel tempted to discount, do it differently. Instead of devaluing what you offer, add value by maintaining your usual prices but throwing in some additional extras. For example, you might offer wine with dinner, special behind-the-scenes tours to a local attraction, or you could show a friendly welcome by doing a deal with a local pub and telling guests that their first drinks there will be on you.

This is the time to demonstrate the real benefits of what you have to offer. Visitor attractions in your area are also likely to suffer if you lose business, so perhaps you can work together to offer something extra and unusual that could attract media interest?

If you have some spare capacity in your accommodation, make sure you offer your best rooms to the guests who do still come, regardless of whether they have paid upgrades and top rates. You need them to go home with very positive reviews of their stay.

Maintaining good relationships with the media

Marketing
- POSTPONE YOUR MARKETING
- ADDED VALUE
- OFFER OTHER OPTIONS
- RE-THINK YOUR TARGET MARKETS

### OFFER OTHER OPTIONS

If you know there are particular concerns that you need to overcome, you can often do this by offering direct solutions. For example, during security alerts at London stations, some hoteliers focused on other ways of reaching them such as by river boat or offering walking routes. During the foot-and-mouth disease crisis when walkers were not allowed across much of the farmland in the Lake District, some hoteliers offered indoor pampering weekends instead.

### RE-THINK YOUR TARGET MARKETS

When one market fails, there is nearly always another to replace it. Think laterally about the segments that you might still be able to attract. You might need to shift your focus from international markets to domestic visitors.

# Chapter 12
# Additional information

## Tourist boards and Destination Management Organisations

VisitBritain
Thames Tower
Blacks Road
London
W6 9EL

Tel: 020 8846 9000

VisitBritain consumer website:
**www.visitbritain.com**
VisitBritain corporate website:
**www.visitbritain.com/corporate**
VisitBritain industry website:
**www.visitbritain.com/ukindustry**
EnjoyEngland domestic consumer website:
**www.enjoyengland.com**

VisitBritain provides a range of statistics, research, intelligence and insights about the domestic and inbound tourism industry at **www.visitbritain.com/research**. Other tourist board research resources include the websites **www.staruk.org.uk** and **www.insights.org.uk**.

Some regional tourist boards are still undergoing changes and new Destination Management Organisations are being established. You can find the latest contacts and details about the national and regional tourist boards on **www.visitbritain.com/ukindustry**.

**Northumbria**
One NorthEast Tourism Team
**www.tourismnortheast.co.uk**

**North West**
Cumbria Tourist Board
**www.cumbriatourism.info**

Lancashire & Blackpool Tourist Board
**www.visitlancashire.com**

Marketing Manchester
**www.visitmanchester.com**

The Mersey Partnership
**www.visitliverpool.com**

Cheshire & Warrington Tourism Board
**www.visit-cheshire.com**

**Yorkshire**
Yorkshire Tourist Board
**www.yorkshiretouristboard.net**

**East Midlands**
East Midlands Tourism
**www.emda.org.uk/tourism/tourism**

**West Midlands**
Heart of England Tourism
**www.visitheartofengland.com**

**East of England**
East of England Tourist Board
**www.eetb.org.uk**

**London**
Visit London
**www.visitlondon.com**

**South East**
Tourism South East
**www.visitsoutheastengland.com**

## South West
South West Tourism
**www.swtourism.co.uk**

Tourist boards and
Destination
Management
Organisations

– SUSTAINABLE
  TOURISM

Northern Ireland Tourist Board consumer website:
**www.discovernorthernireland.com**
Northern Ireland Tourist Board tourism industry website:
**www.nitb.com**

VisitScotland consumer website: **www.visitscotland.com**
Scottish tourism industry website: **www.scotexchange.net**

VisitWales consumer website: **www.visitwales.com**
VisitWales industry website:
**www.industry.visitwales.co.uk**

VisitLondon consumer website: **www.visitlondon.com**
VisitLondon industry website:
**www.visitlondon.com/corporate**

The VisitBritain industry website has details of current
research, statistics and trends at
**www.visitbritain.com/ukindustry**.
You can also find more information on **www.staruk.org.uk**.

Keep up to date with the latest trends and business ideas by
subscribing to free newsletters on sites such as
**www.springwise.com** and **www.trendwatching.com**.

UKinbound represents the interests of companies deriving a
substantial part of their income from the provision of tours
and tourism services for overseas' visitors within Britain
**www.ukinbound.org**.

### SUSTAINABLE TOURISM
Green tourism is a term used to describe best environmental
practice within the tourism sector. The Green Tourism
Business Scheme asks business to agree to a code of
conduct, and through independent assessment of their
activities, members make a commitment towards reducing
the impact of their business on the environment. For more
details see **www.green-business.co.uk**.

The Green Audit Guide is designed to be used by all types of
tourism businesses. It contains practical ideas to help benefit

from the attraction of the countryside, at the same time as contributing to the local community and economy and protecting the environment. A free copy can be downloaded from **www.greenauditkit.org**.

## Accessibility and disability matters

**www.disability.gov.uk**    Official government site for disability matters

**www.drc-gb.org**    Disability Rights Commission

**www.radar.org.uk**    The Disability network

**www.holidaycare.org.uk**    Holiday Care Service

**www.tourismforall.org.uk**    Tourism for All

**www.rnib.org.uk**    Royal National Institute of the Blind

**www.rnid.org.uk**    RNID – representing the deaf and hard of hearing

**Tourism For All** works to create, develop and support an accessible hospitality and tourism industry in the UK and Europe, for customers and staff, regardless of age, disability or income. They also offer advice and training for the tourism industry to aid compliance with the DDA.

Tel: 0845 124 9974
**www.tourismforall.org.uk**

## Business support information and advice

### TAX ISSUES

Contact the **Inland Revenue**. Their Employer's Helpline on 08457 143 143 offers general advice on PAYE, National Insurance, statutory sick pay, maternity pay and tax credits. The Business Support Teams on 0845 60 70 143 offer help and advice specifically for small businesses.

**www.inlandrevenue.gov.uk/employers**

### VALUE ADDED TAX (VAT)

HM Customs and Excise deals with all VAT issues and also run short seminars on VAT for small and new businesses.

Tel: 0845 010 9000
**www.hmce.gov.uk**

## BUSINESS LINK

Business Link is a government-funded agency set up to support small- to medium-sized businesses. It has a wide range of information to help you run your business. Most of the regulatory forms and leaflets needed by businesses can be accessed through the website. Business Link also provides advice on recruitment, employment and disputes.

Business Link has an excellent tool on their website which provides you with a list of licences and permits that your business requires, after answering a few questions. It provides a checklist and local contact details of organisations.

Tel: 0845 600 9006

**www.businesslink.gov.uk**

## Legislation

### EXPANSION OF THE DISCRIMINATION LAWS

In October 2006, Age Discrimination legislation comes into force. For the first time in England, it will be unlawful to discriminate against employees and job applicants on the basis of age. This will affect recruitment, dismissal, pay and benefits, training, redundancy, pensions and retirement.

Last October the final phases of the Disability Discrimination Act (DDA) came into force. Service providers now have to make reasonable adjustments to the physical features of service premises to overcome physical barriers to access.

Equal Opportunities is now a broad and sometimes confusing area, and one in which it pays to get some proper training and advice.

More info from:
The Equal Opportunities Commission – **www.eoc.org.uk**;
The Commission for Racial Equality – **www.cre.gov.uk**;
The Disability Rights Commission – **www.drc.gb.org**.

### DATA PROTECTION

All businesses that keep any kind of record about 'living identifiable people' must comply with the Data Protection Act. The Act applies to any personal information kept electronically and to some extent paper-based records. Some businesses need to register under the Act and ensure that their information is properly managed. But others need only to observe the principles of data protection.

Failure to register with the Information Commissioner's Office or to comply with an enforcement notice is a criminal offence and punishable by a fine. An individual may also seek compensation through the courts for damage suffered if you mismanage their personal information.

### THE PRIVACY DIRECTIVE

The Privacy Directive applies to any business that direct markets by phone, fax, E-mail or SMS to individuals or businesses. It also covers the use of cookies and other internet tracking devices.

For example, businesses are only permitted to send marketing E-mails and SMS messages to individuals who have previously consented to the use of their details in this way. However, there are no restrictions on sending E-mails to business addresses. Firms that ignore this law face a fine of £5,000. This legislation is also enforced by the Information Commissioner's Office.

Information Commissioner's Office Helpline:
Tel: (01625) 545745
**www.informationcommissioner.gov.uk**.

### HEALTH AND SAFETY

The Health and Safety Executive has a confidential helpline and their site includes comprehensive information for the industry. They also publish the Health and Safety Starter Pack which is available via their website, as well as information on school trips and risk assessment measures.

Tel: 0845 345 0055
**www.hse.gov.uk** or **www.hse.gov.uk/catering**

### PEOPLE 1ST

People 1st is the new Sector Skills Council for the hospitality, leisure, travel and tourism industry. Their role is to be the voice of this industry, representing employers' views on skills issues, helping to direct existing government and industry funding where it will do most good, developing the right standards for qualifications, producing information on skills to help businesses, and signposting and promoting the most suitable training and training providers.

People 1st's mission for the next five years is to have an impact on increased completion rates for qualifications and learning programmes, investment in training, employee skills levels, productivity levels and reduced staff turnover.

www.people1st.co.uk

Legislation

– EXPANSION OF THE DISCRIMINATION LAWS
– DATA PROTECTION
– THE PRIVACY DIRECTIVE
– HEALTH AND SAFETY
– PEOPLE 1ST

## Glossary of tourism industry terminology

The tourism and marketing industry is notorious for its range of acronyms and jargon – here's a list of some of them.

**above the line promotion**   Traditionally used to mean commission-based advertising, such as TV, radio, posters and press.

**activity holidays**   One of the fastest-growing sectors of tourism, ranging from relatively leisurely activities such as walking to mountaineering and more extreme sports.

**allocation**   A block booking of hotel rooms or airline seats by an operator or agent, who can then call on that allocation without having to keep re-checking availability with the hotel or airline, until a specified release date.

**below the line promotion**   Traditionally used to mean print-based promotional activities for which commission is not paid, such as brochures and direct mail. Below the line promotion generally seeks to build a relationship with the consumer.

**benchmarking**   Process of comparing performance and activities among similar organisations, either against an agreed standard or against those that are recognised as being among the best.

**business travel**   Travel for commerce rather than pleasure.

**confidential tariff**   Discounted prices quoted to wholesalers, tour operators and travel agents, distributed in confidence and not published for public use.

**consolidator**   A company or individual that brings together different groups of people on air charters or at group rates on scheduled flights to increase sales, earn override commissions or reduce the possibility of tour cancellations.

**convention *or* conference bureau**   Usually a publicly funded organisation charged with the promotion of a town or region for conferences, meetings and exhibitions.

**day visitors**   Visitors who arrive and leave the same day, irrespective of why they are travelling.

**Destination Management Company (*or* DMC)**
Company that handles all bookings and arrangements for tours or conferences in a specific destination. Tour operators or conference planners are likely to use the services of a DMC because of their specialist local knowledge.

**Destination Marketing Organisation (*or* DMO)**
Company or consortia (often a public/private partnership) responsible for the promotion of a specific area or town. DMOs are becoming increasingly popular in the UK.

**domestic tourism**   UK residents travelling within the country itself.

**dwell time**   Length of time visitors spend at an attraction. Dwell time is often taken into consideration when setting admission fees as a way of ensuring value for money.

**ecotourism**   Defined by The International Ecotourism Society as 'responsible travel to natural areas that conserves the environment and sustains the well-being of local people'.

**familiarisation *or* fam. trip**   Free or reduced-rate trip usually for tour operators, travel agents or journalists so they can experience a destination or tourism product first hand and then promote it.

**ground operator *or* ground handler**   Company making all arrangements for incoming groups or travellers from overseas, from the moment they arrive in the UK (or other destination) to the moment they leave the country. This may include anything from accommodation booking to arranging sightseeing tours.

**incentive tour/trip** Once-in-a-lifetime experience or trip, usually offered to either stimulate sales staff to sell more or as a reward for increased sales activity.

**incoming** *or* **inbound tourism** Refers to visitors from other countries coming to the UK.

**incoming tour operator** Incoming tour operators essentially offer the same services as ground handlers, although they are more likely to offer their own programmes and not just react to clients' demands.

**leisure tourist/visitor** Travelling for pleasure not business, including those who travel in order to visit friends and relatives.

**length of stay** Number of nights spent in one destination. Most tourist boards seek to find ways of increasing visitors' length of stay.

**MICE** Umbrella term referring to several aspects of business tourism: Meetings Incentives Conventions and Exhibitions.

**net rate** The price for hotel rooms, car hire or other products before they are 'marked up' with an additional margin for profit for sale to the public.

**occupancy rate** Refers to the number of rooms or beds occupied by guests on any given date, usually presented as a percentage. Because accommodation is perishable (i.e. if rooms are unsold on the 1st December, there will not be another chance to sell them), high occupancy rates are essential to profitability.

**package tour** A travel product (often sold by travel agents or direct 'off the page') with an inclusive price covering the different elements of the trip, for example, transport to the destination, accommodation, catering and perhaps some sightseeing activities.

**pax** Shorthand for passengers.

**rack rate** The official rate advertised by a hotel or other tourism provider. This is the 'rate across the counter', in other words, the one offered to the public, before any discounts are applied.

**sustainable tourism**   According to the World Tourism Organisation, this is 'envisaged as leading to management of all resources in such a way that economic, social and aesthetic needs can be fulfilled whilst maintaining cultural integrity, essential ecological processes, biological diversity and life support systems'.

**VFR**   An important segment in tourism although often ignored, VFR stands for Visiting Friends and Relatives.

**wholesaler**   A company that does not sell to the public but through travel agents and particularly tour and coach operators. They generally rely on low-margin, mass-market products.

**yield management**   A practice pioneered by airlines and now used by accommodation providers and other tourism suppliers to maximise revenue by raising or lowering prices according to demand.

## Key tourism industry organisations

### Association for Conferences and Events
The largest membership organisation in the meetings industry based in the UK.

**www.martex.co.uk/ace**

### Association of British Travel Agents (ABTA)
The UK's largest travel trade organisation, representing more than 2,200 agents and tour operators.

**www.abta.com**

### British Holiday and Home Parks Association
BH & HPA is the representative body of the parks industry including caravans, chalets, tents and all types of self-catering park accommodation.

**www.ukparks.com**

### British Hospitality Association
The BHA is the largest and most influential trade association in the hotel and catering sector and has some 22,000 members. Its hotel membership is drawn mainly from the middle and upper end of the market.

**www.bha-online.org.uk**

## British Institute of Innkeeping

The BII is the professional body for the licensed trade, promoting high standards of professionalism throughout the licensed retail sector.

www.bii.org.uk

## British Resorts Association

Represents the interest of resorts throughout the UK, including both seaside and inland resorts.

www.britishresorts.co.uk

## The Camping and Caravanning Club (CCC)

One of the largest clubs in the world and the second largest operator of campsites in the world.

www.campingandcaravanningclub.co.uk

## The Caravan Club

Represents the interests of over 800,000 caravanners with a nationwide network of quality sites.

www.caravanclub.co.uk

## Department for Culture, Media and Sport

The government department responsible for tourism.

www.culture.gov.uk

## English Association of Self-Catering Operators

Trade body for operators of self-catering holiday flats, apartments, etc.

www.englishselfcatering.co.uk

## Foreign and Commonwealth Office

www.fco.gov.uk

## Hotel and Catering International Management Association (HCIMA)

Professional body for managers and potential managers in the hospitality industry, covering hotels, contract catering, restaurants and pubs to hospitals', schools' and armed forces' catering.

www.hcima.org.uk

### Institute of Travel and Tourism
The professional body for the travel and tourism industry offering membership to appropriately qualified individuals.

**www.itt.co.uk**

### Restaurant Association
The Restaurant Association is the voice for the industry on regulatory issues and government initiatives where appropriate.

**www.restaurant.org**

### Tourism Alliance
Members of the Tourism Alliance comprise leading trade associations and trade bodies within the sector. Its main purpose is to lobby government on the key strategic issues facing the industry.

**www.tourismalliance.com**

### Tourism Management Institute
Membership organisation for tourism officers from local authorities, regional and national tourist organisations and other companies involved in tourism.

**www.tmi.org.uk**

### The Tourism Network
A not-for-profit industry support agency offering training, networking opportunities and consultancy for tourism professionals in the UK, aimed at making their job easier and more fun.

**www.tourismnetwork.org**

### Tourism Society
Membership body that aims to promote and enhance professionalism in tourism. Tourism-related training meetings held throughout the year.

**www.tourismsociety.org**

# Index